What's in the Closet?

Fern Jinkins

This creative non-fiction book comes from the memories contained in life experiences. It is in no way meant to hurt any person, living or dead but simply a story of overcoming difficult circumstances and finding healing through Jesus Christ. To that end, the names of characters portrayed in this book were changed with the exceptions of the author/primary character and her sons. Places mentioned do exist and these events happened. We added dialogue and actions based on what may have been said and done, taking a degree of creative license to make this book more interesting and touching for the readers.

To my loving mother, Carol Sue Simpson, a resident of Heaven. May she rest in peace until we meet again someday.

Table of Contents

ACKNOWLEDGEMENTS

Willie E. Jinkins, my loving husband. Words cannot express the gratitude in my heart. You stood beside me and loved me when I didn't understand what true love looked like. You are a big reason I now understand the kind of love God gives without condition. Through the entire process of writing this book, you remained my champion and constant encouragement. Thank you for loving me, just the way I am.

To my sons, Corey R. Smith, Isaiah Reed and Trenton Spears, you taught me what God's love looks like and how to live it. You accepted me and never gave up on me through the many trials. In spite of what I did, you all became wonderful young men of whom I am very proud.

Thank you to the many pastors, ministers and friends who believed in me when I didn't believe in myself. Many of you stuck by me even when I failed and while I journeyed through the process of healing. Without you, how could I succeed and walk in faith as the woman God intended me to become?

And finally, to my editor and publisher, Lisa Bell of Radical Women, thank you for taking on this project. You took my thoughts, memories and emotions and so eloquently wrote the words I wanted to convey, but couldn't find. Thank you for making this book a reality and tool that now God can use.

Above all, I thank my Lord and Savior, Jesus Christ. Without Him, I wouldn't have a story worth sharing or a life worth living. To Him be all the glory and honor.

Foreword

Fern,

Congratulations on the release of your new book! I'm not at all surprised by this rendition of your faith unleashed. In the 25 plus years I've known you, I've watched your faith multiply through both victory and trial. I've known your determination to be all of what God prepared for you before you were born. Your faith-filled tenacity and willingness to share your journey with the world is evidence of true evangelism. Thank you for sharing the transforming truth of the Gospel. It is my earnest prayer that all who read *What's in the Closet?*" are thoroughly transformed as they are led to God's love and His saving grace, Jesus Christ.

Coyletta Govan,
Founder/Executive Director at DFW CITIWomen
Cornerstone Assistance Network Promise House Coordinator

I remember getting a call from this young lady over seven years ago. I knew of her from us going to the same Church, The Potter's House of Fort Worth, but I didn't know anything about her. I didn't know her personally, but she reached out to know me.

I recall that I agreed to meet her at Chill's Restaurant on a nice sunny day in the month of October. After a warm greeting and fellowship, we ordered our food, eating lightly because there was much for her to tell me. The conversation started with her sharing her life struggles and an addiction she desired to overcome. She requested that I become a "Spiritual Mentor," revealing God directed her to reach out to me.

Well...after she finished sharing, I was not surprised or shocked because of my experience in crisis with others I walked alongside. I accepted this journey with her under the disclaimer, "I will not waste my time or energy in minds games." And if God sent her, then I would be the strength she needed.

Now, here we are still together seven years later. I believe she has been on a seven-years cleaning in foremost her spirit. Because of her being a strong believer, it was hard for her to accept that if she was so into God and knew his Word like she believed she did, she still struggled. Then my question to her was, "Why is it not working?"

By her beginning to take this spiritual journey with me, she has blossomed into a mighty new creature in Christ Jesus. I statute her effort for putting down her life story so that she can help be a witness of the awesome powers of God's divine protection and deliverances of many shocking things she had to endure as a child, at no fault of her own.

May this book further witness and help bring change to many lives.

Elder Eleanor Pat Miller
Destined to Win Ministries

Introduction

I tried to write this book for several years. I made a decision in 2018 to start writing and trust God in the process. The information I am about to share is very sensitive to me, but my prayer is that it brings enlightenment to others and helps them walk through the vicissitudes of life by accepting Jesus as their personal Lord and Savior.

I was born to the parents of Carol Simpson and Rev. Rogers. I will not disclose his real full name, because it is not on my birth certificate. My mom met my dad when he was married to another woman. In the relationship that followed, they conceived me, which caused a lot of problems for her over the years. Today we will focus on me. May my mother rest in peace.

Chapter 1

On March 3, 1966, I took my first breath with circumstances against me. How could I end up any other way than a mess?

While Mother and Daddy no doubt loved each other, they weren't married. That in and of itself created major issues. As if that wasn't enough, from the very beginning, asthma plagued my tiny body, producing a sickly child.

I remember being in the hospital for most of my childhood. Most times the doctors gave my mom a grim prognosis. "There's nothing more we can do. You may want to prepare for her burial."

Perhaps she considered that as a possibility, but each time I went home. Several times over my life I was hospitalized. Nurses and doctors did nothing more than put me on an ice bed, oxygen tent and nebulizer. I took breathing treatments regularly.

Each time, I rarely had any visitors, so I also felt alone. Fear and a deep sadness filled me. Was this the time I was going to die or lose all my hope? I missed so much school I wondered how to keep up.

The only person that visited me was my mom. I waited in my room, listening for her footstep. Her heels clicked against the floor as she came down the hallway, distinctive and recognizable long before she reached my room. It didn't matter which hospital. I always knew those steps. In spite of the doctors' outlook, she never gave up on me. That still amazes me. We were not Christians, yet it had to be God that saved me from death.

Mom oozed class. Regardless of her bad decisions, I always admired the refined way she carried herself. She always dressed sharp and made sure I had the best material possessions. After she became a drug dealer, things changed because of the environment we lived in. She could be very sweet, kind, giving, offered sound advice and made sure I learned from school and about the streets. Looking at her, no one suspected her as a drug dealer. After her death, I realized she was so hard on me because she did not ever want me to experience the hardships and challenges she had to face as a parent. Some of her behaviors were unethical, but I learned from the best. She did the best she could with the information and choices she had. May God allow her soul to rest in peace.

During my childhood, we moved a lot. Some of the places where I remember living included the Riverside Village, Glen Gardens, on Marion Street, Mulkey, Stuart Drive, Hatcher, Lancaster, Meadowbrook, Weiler Blvd, Motel 6, and other motels in the Metroplex. We lived in several different apartments in the Riverside Village—at least four. My mom was a nurse, which meant she didn't make enough money to support us well.

And that begins my story. Even with all the negative beginnings, I made it to first grade, and then my world really got turned upside down.

Chapter 2

One day, I walked home from school with my sister, Angel. Happy I wasn't sick, I felt almost normal.

At home, a man sat on our front steps. I knew him, but not well.

"Hi, Fern," Malik said. "Your mom isn't here, so you and your sister will be living with us for a while."

"What? Where's Mom? Is she okay?" My mind raced with all the possible scenarios.

"She's in prison." Flat. To the point—no emotion.

That wasn't one of the scenarios I imagined. Fear rose up and spilled out of my eyes in the form of tears. Confusion fueled them. Why didn't Mom tell us what was going on? I had no idea this was coming, and neither did Angel. How could she let this happen and not prepare us? And what would happen to us? I didn't know Malik, but I knew he was someone that came to my mom after she got involved with all the drugs. I didn't like it when she had drugs around, although she tried to keep it hidden from us. Even as a young child I wasn't stupid.

Malik took our hands. "C'mon. We gotta get all your stuff."

At our new "home," Malik and his brother spent a good

deal of their time doing drugs. Mom joined a Muslim group at the prison, which allowed her to visit us on the weekends. But she didn't stop any of the stuff going on.

One day, I played in the bedroom alone. Being alone didn't bother me much. I'd experienced it for most of my life because of illness and the many hospital visits. The door opened and Malik's nephew slinked into the room, closing the door behind him.

He suggested playing doctor with me. But soon the game changed to something unlike I'd ever known from any doctor, and I didn't like it. Not one bit.

Suddenly, the door opened and his mother stepped into the room. She grabbed her son by the arm. "Get out of here now."

He didn't even respond, but zipped up his pants and left the room.

She turned to me. "Don't you ever do that again." The ice in her voice made chills run all over me. What did I do? I didn't want to play his game, and it was all his idea anyway. Why did I feel like it was my fault?

But none of that came out of my mouth. "Yes, ma'am." She turned and slammed the door behind her. I adjusted my clothes, curled up in a ball and wept.

Although this boy didn't actually molest me, I feared he would try again. And I instinctively knew this wasn't right. Did I somehow cause the unwanted attention? I was just a little girl, but at the moment I knew only guilt. I'd be more careful. Not only was the situation bad, but it could be worse. If I did it again, the mother in this house might put us out. And then what?

I'm not sure which scared me more—the thought of being put out of the house or staying and risking the abuse of a young man. I sure didn't want him to touch me again, or do even more if he felt like it. But when you're a child you have very little control over what happens to you. Especially if you're already in a bad situation without a mom or dad to protect you from evil.

Chapter 3

Still only an innocent six-year-old, I was completely unprepared for events that haunted me for much of my life.

After those initial days with Malik, we spent several nights with our family. Finally, I thought I could sleep. Family is safe, right? One cousin stands out above all the others. I wasn't sure why Aliyah chose me, but she treated me like I was special. Every day, she paid me attention, something I didn't normally get from anyone.

One night, she came and got me out of bed, pressing a finger to her lips so I wouldn't make any noise. In her bedroom, she moved on top of me with a towel placed between her legs. She hunched against the towel and rubbed my body, touching places no one ever touched. I didn't know what to do, so I lay there letting Aliyah do what she wanted. When she finished with me, she sent me back to my own bed.

"This is our secret. Don't tell anyone," she said. "You're my special little girl."

I returned to my bed and cried softly into my pillow, not sure why. Something about the whole ordeal didn't feel right.

The same thing happened many times, sometimes even

during the day on the floor of the master bedroom. The air-conditioner blew across us as she performed her version of sex on me. At times, her parents were home, but no one ever came in and stopped us. She was my older cousin, so although I didn't understand what was happening, why my body reacted in certain ways or what I felt, I figured it must be okay. No one stopped her. And I never told anyone—not even my sister.

One day, Aliyah came up to me. "Wanna go see my boyfriend with me?"

What an honor. I didn't usually get to go anywhere except school. I must be special. But when we got there, I wasn't sure what to think.

"Watch and learn," she said.

The two of them led me to his bedroom where they had sex, acting oblivious to my presence. When they finished, I couldn't get out of the house fast enough. Back at our house, she took me into the bedroom and closed the door. She did things to me that day I'd seen while she was with her boyfriend.

I still didn't understand why or what was happening. She must really love me and think me special. Yet every night I cried silently alone in my bed. I couldn't share the things my cousin did—not even with Angel.

Aliyah had to go out one day, but her mom was still at work. She invited her friend, Xavier, over to the house.

"Watch her for me." Aliyah winked. "You can do anything you want with her. She won't tell anyone." With that, she smiled a crooked grin, twitched her eyebrows, and then walked out of the house.

"Hey, pipsqueak, let's have some fun," Xavier said. "C'mon in the bedroom."

He pulled me onto the bed and then got on top of me. I was used to this because of Aliyah, but this time felt different.

There wasn't a towel involved, but he used his body, making the same movements she did. Without the towel, the sensations were similar. I had never seen a naked boy before, so I didn't understand the difference in body parts. Although he didn't penetrate me, he still satisfied himself with my body.

I no longer liked being at my Aunt's house, but what else could I do? Even when Mom got out of prison, we couldn't live with her. She visited sometimes, but I never told her all the things going on with our cousins. Always a promise we'd be together soon, Mom left each time with me wishing to go with her. Nothing could be as bad as our "home." Afterward, even our aunt and uncle talked bad about her, calling her worthless with accusations about abandoning her children with them. My sister and I sat in shame listening to their hurtful words. Guilt and shame washed over me, even as a child. I tried to behave so I wasn't a burden to them. Still, I wasn't really welcome— nothing more than a plaything for my one cousin who took delight in using me for her own pleasure.

The things going on with my cousin were bad enough, but for some reason when my aunt went to work, they'd get my sister and me and put us in a closet, locking the door behind us. "Get in there, scallywags." I had no idea what scallywag meant, but I knew it wasn't good.

Each time the lock clicked, I knew it meant nothing to eat or drink. For hours we sat in the closet. I tried not to cry, but sobs soon took control of me.

Angel wrapped her arms around me. "It'll be okay, Fern. It'll be okay."

But as hunger gnawed at my belly and the thirst became overwhelming, the darkness grew stronger. After a while, though, I tuned out those feelings. Sometimes, the closet became my friend. Angel and I were safe in the closet. No one touched me inappropriately. No one hurt me. In the closet, a strange sense of safety comforted me.

At times they opened up the door. "Fern, c'mon out here."

I grabbed Angel's hand, ready for the two of us to get some freedom and maybe a little food.

"Not her. Just you."

I hated it when they said those words. I learned quickly what came next.

"Okay, kid. Call your sister black. She's so dark and ugly. She's such a scallywag. Tell her."

I shook my head as fresh tears formed. I didn't want to call my sister bad names. I loved her.

"Tell her." Anger filled their words. "Or we'll put you back in there."

The tears broke loose, not because of their threats, but because they made me be mean to her. Why did they want to play this nasty game? I didn't understand.

"Call her those names you scallywag."

They kept up the game until I finally gave in, sobbing through the words coming out of my mouth. Finally, they grew tired, opened the door and shoved me back into the closet.

"I'm so sorry." The sobs shook my whole body.

"It's okay, baby. I know you didn't mean it. It's okay." Angel soothed me with her hugs and tender touch. "Shhhh. It's gonna be okay."

But was it? How could it ever be okay without Mom to take care of us? Just before time for my aunt to come home, they opened up the closet and told us both to come out and get cleaned up. We never told Auntie what her kids did to us— none of it. Maybe they threatened to make things worse if we did. I'm not sure. But we didn't dare tell her anything.

I didn't think it could get any worse than life already felt.

But my nightmare hadn't reached the worst parts yet, and I didn't even know how bad things could get.

Chapter 4

Aliyah continued her use of my body, but that wasn't enough for her. One day she introduced me to her boyfriend's brother.

"Ooh, you're gonna like having your own boyfriend," she told me. "Dajon's gonna do wonderful things to you."

He took me into a bedroom. I prepared myself for the things to come, thinking I knew. I'd experienced the difference between girls and boys after all. This time felt completely different.

As he moved on top of me and starting using his body parts, extreme pain shot through me.

"That hurts. Please stop," I screamed.

"No, it doesn't. Just be quiet and relax."

"No. It hurts so bad. Please." I begged as every time he moved hurt worse. The pain overwhelmed me. I kept pleading with him to stop. But Dajon thrust more and more, paying me no attention.

To shut out the pain, I willed my mind to go somewhere else—anywhere. Even through the tears, I managed to take myself out of the situation, tuning out what this boy did. It was the first time my mind didn't stay in the immediate happenings.

When he finally finished, I lay there crying softly, between my legs hurting worse than anything I ever felt before. After several minutes I got up and went to the bathroom. When I wiped, blood stained the toilet tissue. I started in disbelief. Why was I bleeding down there? My hands shook while I pulled up my panties.

Aliyah met me in the hallway. "Well, how'd you like it, kid?"

My voice came out in a whisper. "I'm bleeding down there."

"Cool. Now you're really a big girl. Did you enjoy it? I bet you did."

What if I said no? What if I admitted I hated every minute of the torturous pain and the fear that came with it? I nodded slightly, afraid of what they would do if I told the truth.

Over the years, he became my boyfriend having sex with me whenever he chose, whether I wanted it or not. Eventually, he took me to the school prom, even though I was much younger than him. It was my mom, though, who bought the mum for me. The beautiful flowers didn't hide the scars in my soul. I never told her what he'd been doing to me for years. I figured she knew anyway—that it was normal for a boy and girl to have sex even at a young age. It must be okay since I experienced it so many times before I ever got to high school.

Finally, Mom got out of prison, and for a change, we got to live with her. Unfortunately, she came with Buster, maybe her way to have a decent place to live. I'm not sure why she dated him. From the very beginning, my stomach roiled at the very sight of this man. He was big, ugly and scary-looking— especially to a little girl.

Mom worked nights a lot. And Buster took advantage of it.

Sometimes he hit Angel and argued with our mother. When Mom was away, the scarier part of Buster came out. Although Angel didn't know about the sexual abuse I already endured, she protected me from this man. Not from total willingness, she gave herself to him whenever he wanted sex. He physically hurt her in so many ways, but he never came after me.

Because Mom worked at night, we became easy targets for any predator—sick men who wanted little girls along with or instead of grown women. What is wrong with such a man? I never understood why Buster desired sex with Angel, but he enjoyed taking advantage of her. I sometimes heard her crying during and after those times. The more she told him it hurt, the rougher he seemed to get.

Angel and I didn't talk about what he did, and we sure didn't tell Mom. Were there threats from him? I don't remember. But maybe it came unspoken. The beatings Angel took and I saw were enough to keep us more than silent.

I don't think Mom knew what was going on. She sold some weed on the side, but at that point, she wasn't deep into the drug world. His place was decent, but at the same time, she and Buster fought a lot as well. He didn't have a problem hitting her either.

One night they got into a huge argument. Initially, he was downstairs, and she was upstairs. But the whole neighborhood could hear the ruckus. Angel and I hid in the bedroom, trying to stay out of the way, terrified at what he might do to us. When he got that angry, his fists didn't care where they landed. So we stayed out of the way.

Somehow, Mom ended up outside as Buster revved up his car engine. Angel and I watched through the window. Still screaming at each other, he aimed his vehicle at her and ran her down, hitting her body so hard she flew past the two-story building next door.

"No!" Angel and I both yelled, certain he killed her.

When they released her from the hospital, we went to live with relatives yet again. My aunt wasn't so bad, but the rest of the family treated us like dirt, locking us in the closet and calling us names. I could deal with that, but I hated it when they talked about Mom as if we couldn't hear. They had nothing good to say about her. Good or bad, right or wrong, she was my mother, even if she wasn't there most of the time.

Eventually, she came back to get us. And for a while, I thought everything was gonna be okay. It had to be better. At least we weren't going back to Buster's place and for that I was thankful. For once in my life, maybe, just maybe life could be good.

Chapter 5

I've never been so glad to get away from someone. Buster terrified me. I hated living with relatives who didn't seem to want us around much. And I missed Mom.

When she met another man, Jay, and started dating him I wasn't sure how to feel. Would he be another Buster? I certainly hoped not.

Before long we all moved in with him. I liked Jay. He bought us things we never had before. He treated us well, never locking me in a closet, and his house was one of the nicest places I ever lived. For the first time, I felt safe with plenty of food, toys and everything I could possibly want. It was almost like a dream there. And I never wanted it to end.

But who was I to hope for a good life? Even at my young age, most of my memories weren't very good. Still, things looked better, and finally, I had hope of a life like kids I knew from school. He wasn't great to Angel, sometimes hitting on her. But he didn't hurt her the way Buster did, at least not as far as I knew. I felt bad for my sister, yet glad we had a better life.

Then one night, the goodness turned ugly.

Jay and I watched TV together. I always liked it when he

invited me to come and sit with him. Sometimes he let me pick the show, and usually, we'd have a snack too. For some reason, Mom and Angel weren't home that night.

"Fern, I wanna show you something. Pull down your panties for me."

"What?"

"C'mon, girl. You know I ain't gonna hurt you. It'll feel good."

As I think back on that night, the memories blur, yet somehow they remain vivid in my mind, haunting me with shame and sorrow. Jay unzipped his pants and rubbed himself between my legs. Then he put his mouth on my private parts and licked me very slowly.

What was he doing? I was clueless. In everything that happened to me before that night, no one had ever performed oral sex on me. And I wasn't interested in learning about it from this man I trusted like a father. But he didn't stop.

After a while, he put his private part between my legs again and rubbed it against my body. Thankful he didn't enter me, I still wanted to cry. My mind searched for the closet, a safe place to be away from the abuse. In a short time, he stood up and walked to the bathroom, sperm dripping all along the way.

When he returned, Jay mumbled something. My mind couldn't comprehend the words, still numb from the fresh round of betrayal. But I sensed it was something along the lines of how good that was and not to tell anyone. No one would understand, and they wouldn't let us be together anymore.

That was the first night, but it certainly wasn't the last. Every chance he got, Jay repeated his ritual. Calling me to him and demanding I remove my panties. As time went on, he graduated from rubbing against my legs and vagina to full-blown sex, both oral and physical.

Most of the time, my mind sought refuge in a mental closet. I blocked out everything around me, even which shows we watched. When this sick man finished, I'd come back to my senses, redress and both of us went on with the night as if nothing happened. What else can you do from the time you are 6 years old until you turn 11?

Besides, who would believe me? Jay was slick, the perfect father-figure. People always commented on how good he was to me and Angel—how he took care of us like we were his own daughters. I didn't know how most fathers treated their daughters, but I didn't hear any of my friends talking about nightly excursions on the sofa with their dads.

I shook inside all the time, filled with fear of this monster. Yet he gave us a good home, and I was away from Aliyah most of the time. At least he didn't lock me in the closet with nothing to eat or drink. If I said anything, would he put us out? Maybe I was wrong, and this was how it was supposed to be, but I didn't think so.

One of my respites from everything came from a place called the Palace. I loved the lady who owned this skating rink. She always treated Angel, me and the other kids so nice. Sometimes she even invited us to her home. At first, I feared going there and what might happen. But it was the one place where I truly felt safe. It was the best place of all my childhood—the one place of freedom from the terrible things elsewhere.

One night Jay showed up to take me home. "Look what I got, Fern." He held out a magazine with naked people on and in it. "Take a look and see what looks like fun. We can experiment with anything you want to try."

I looked at a picture, which depicted things he wanted to try. I didn't like the looks of any of it. I screamed at him. A stream of expletives uncommon to a little girl flew from my mouth. The car stopped near a wooded area with a trail. I jumped out, still screaming, and walked along the trail. What could happen to me worse than he was already doing?

All the way home, I cried, questions washing over me like the tears coming from my eyes. Why did Jay always want to have sex with me? Wasn't Mom enough for him? I knew they had sex—I could hear them some nights. She sounded as if it was enjoyable for her. I didn't get it. I hated sex with him.

A thought occurred to me. Did Mom know? Did she care? What would happen if I told her what Jay did to me? She might blame me. Doubts rolled across my brain. Maybe it was my fault. The way I dressed or acted. Did that make him want me? Was I asking for it without even realizing it? After all, I had a history with Aliyah and Dajon. Maybe some part of me wanted this from Jay. But I was still just a little kid, and he was a man. A drug-dealing, player kind of man.

I had no idea what to do.

At home, Jay met me outside. The glare in his eyes pierced through to my bones. "You better not tell your mom or something bad will happen to you both."

My throat seized, but I managed to nod. I'd seen Jay's temper. Although he never used it on me, he hit Angel quite frequently. One blow and I'd probably be dead. And he wouldn't hesitate to kill Mom, or something worse. I wasn't taking that chance. I kept my mouth shut.

Jay kept preying on me, still a child, but not so innocent. Each time, my mind found its closet, tucked my thought process inside and shut the door. I couldn't hear the TV or any other sound. My body froze, unable to move. Yet over time, involuntary reactions took over producing sensations I never knew before. Even then I couldn't move. I wanted to scream, beg him to stop, but my voice stayed in the closet with my mind.

One night in particular, he finished with me and walked to the back of the house. As my mind and body slowly crept from the closet, a knock rang against the door and a guy called Red let himself in.

"Hey, kid. Where's Jay?" Red looked at me. "You OK?"

I stared at his face. I saw this man before—probably one of Jay's dealers—but I didn't really know him. What if I told him the truth? What if I said, "No, I'm NOT. And I haven't been since your friend started messing with me." But if I told him, he might think he could do the same. Or worse, Jay might get rough with me and hurt me more. He might kill me—or Angel and Mom.

I just sat there wanting to cry, but holding back the tears and saying nothing.

For years, I dreaded nights alone with Jay. And they were frequent. I wasn't sure if he did things with Angel or not. In my own world of pain and isolation, I had a hard time thinking past getting into and out of my secret mind closet.

By the time I turned 11, I figured out screaming or cussing out a person tended to make them leave you alone. It didn't work much with Jay, but with everyone else, I developed a way to protect myself to some extent. Verbal abuse of others made some of them turn away, even if it didn't work all the time.

Isolation became my closest friend. Even Mom helped with that.

As a much younger child, I liked talking to my mom. Sometimes she got tired of listening to me. She'd open up the pantry and put me under one of the shelves. "You talk too much. When you're ready to be quiet, I'll let you out."

Being in the closet with Angel wasn't so bad. At least she

comforted me and made me feel safe. But without her, fear slithered over me. I pretended other people were there with me. Having friends in that closet made me feel safer. Then one day, I saw people in the closet beside me, maybe even whispering. But mostly they moved around me, never touching me.

I had to protect myself. My mind was going haywire. So I closed my eyes, and they disappeared. If I couldn't see them, they couldn't hurt me. To be honest, I came to like the closet. Alone with no one to hurt me, call me names or make me feel dirty and ashamed because of what they did with my body. For years I could sit in a dark house or closet by myself and feel safer than being around other people.

All those years with Jay, Mom kept planning to rob him for his drugs and get us out of there. I don't think she knew what he did with us while she worked, but for some reason, she wanted a place of our own. And she found one at Riverside Village.

Finally, freedom.

With Jay gone, maybe everything would be better. In our own place, I didn't worry about another man molesting me. And surely things had to get better.

Chapter 6

The Riverside Village was a drug-infested, gang-related, hustling complex. Everything possibly illegal happened in The Riverside Village. And then there was Rachel.

Rachel lived next door. She welcomed me to the neighborhood. Although a little skeptical, I trusted her. So when she asked to spend the night, I checked with Mom and told her to come on over.

Without an extra room, we shared my bed. I didn't think anything of it. But before long, she started rubbing my body. At first, I thought of it as a friendly gesture, like someone rubbing your back. After several minutes, she got closer to private parts and then started kissing my body as well. Sirens exploded in my brain, but I didn't say anything. I didn't know what to do. Memories of Aliyah flashed like frames of a horror movie.

Then Rachel began performing oral sex. The closet of my mind swung open, beckoning me to escape. My body reacted with a total shutdown. The room disappeared from view and every sound followed behind it. I couldn't see or hear anything, every bad encounter circling over me like vultures.

Her breath lingered against my skin, her tongue moving

slowly all over my body. I wanted to scream or push her off me. But cocooned in the safety of my closet-mind, I remained frozen. Yet, somehow a strange sensation drifted over me. Was some part of me actually feeling good? No. I didn't want this. This was bad. Even in my frozen state, confusion found a way into my brain.

I liked boys, not girls. But maybe I didn't like boys. Boys hurt. As much as I didn't want this with Rachel, it wasn't physically painful. She finally did all she wanted and fell asleep. My mind wouldn't shut down long enough to sleep.

How could I work through all this mess? I couldn't talk to Mom about it. How would she react? Besides, I deserved this. I let Rachel in our house from the beginning. I gave her permission to spend the night and sleep in my bed. I was to blame for all of it. Worst of all, I didn't stop her. I didn't know how to stop Rachel or anyone who ever molested me. Child or not, it had to be my fault.

The next morning, I had no words for my neighbor.

"Thanks for a great night, kid," she said. "I'm going home now."

I simply shrugged my shoulders and turned away from her, waiting until she left. When she didn't go immediately, I slipped out to the bathroom. When I came back, she was gone. I sighed in relief. And then I noticed my secret place for hiding money was in disarray. No one else had been in my room. Even before lifting the top of the box, I knew. The money was gone—all of it. I didn't have that much, but Rachel didn't leave a penny.

Anger shook my body before despair took over. I couldn't do anything about it. Who was I gonna tell? The rest of the truth might slip out if I said anything to anyone.

I wanted to tell my mom, but I wasn't sure how she might react. Selling weed at the time, she always had guns in the house along with the pounds of weed. If I told her what Rachel did to me, would she shoot her or blame me for it all and put me out of the house?

For the first time in a while, I let thoughts of Angel resurface in my mind. I still remembered the night Mom put her out of the house. A massive argument ended with Mom calling my sister "fast." I wasn't sure exactly what that meant, but I knew Angel had a lot of boyfriends. By the time she was 16, Angel graduated to heroin. I used to look at her and see the weariness on her face. The years of protecting me from Buster and trying to keep me away from Jay lined her forehead and eyes long before she reached sweet 16. And by then, all of the trauma squeezed every drop of sweetness from her, at least toward anyone but me.

But Mom didn't know any of that. She just blamed Angel for being in trouble all the time.

I started stealing a little marijuana from Mom's stash, looking for a way to cope with the anxiety and fear I felt toward any man and then even from girls slightly older than me. Just a kid, I already used and sold drugs for my mom. She sometimes put me on a train to Odessa with a briefcase filled with money. I returned with that same briefcase filled with weed. No one suspected a little kid of transporting drugs. Well aware that I was breaking the law, Mom seemed to be fine with it. No wonder I spent most of my childhood completely confused.

Over time my grades began dropping. The teachers and counselors didn't question it so much. I wore such nice clothes to school, they apparently assumed my home life was fine. Since she didn't drive, Mom hired cab drivers to take me everywhere, even to school. Most were okay, as were the three men who worked for Mom, and eventually my stepdad. They never touched me inappropriately.

But one cab driver, Mr. Garcia, was a pedophile. I'm not sure if Mom knew that.

One day, he pulled out a camera and snapped a picture of me. "Strike some poses, girl. You're so cute, I just need a picture or two of you."

I posed innocently. He suggested other moves. I complied. Then it got weird.

"Let me see your cute little breasts."

What?

"C'mon. It's so you can see how you look to the boys."

I wasn't sure exactly what to say or do. He kept telling me to do it. Finally, I did. And he showed me the pictures on his digital camera.

"See. They're really cute." He paused. "You wanna have some fun with me?"

I shook my head. I definitely had no desire to have his kind of fun.

"I bet you already know how to do the whole sex thing. Someone as cute as you and so well-developed." He leaned over the seat. "I'll come back there with you and make you feel real good."

Day after day, he suggested we make a quick stop on the way to school so I could start my day feeling really good.

Each time, I cussed him out and added a few choice names. "You sicko. Pervert." On and on—some names and words I don't care to repeat.

I talked to Mom one morning. "Don't make me ride with Mr. Garcia anymore. I don't like him."

"Oh, he's so nice. Why you don't like him? He's a good man."

Like a wolf, I thought. "Not really." My insides boiled, rising up until they exploded in my words. "I HATE him."

"That's not nice, Fern. Mr. Garcia told me you're mad all the time. I don't know what you have to be mad about. You got a roof over your head and nicer clothes than most of the kids at school." She turned and continued packaging some weed to sell. "You go on now and get in that cab."

Many times we had this conversation, but Mom never once asked why I was so mad—at Mr. Garcia or at the world. She didn't get it, and she probably didn't want to.

I had perfected the ability to isolate myself, never hugging people or saying much. No joy or laughter like what I saw in most of my classmates. Fear crawled around inside of me, keeping me always questioning my dress and actions. Was I to blame for all that people did to me during those first dozen years of my life? The prospect scared me into silence.

And in my mind, I always had my closed-off little closet where I could retreat at a moment's notice. My closet, where I was always safe and nothing could really hurt me.

Chapter 7

The Riverside Village Served as Mom's home-base. I have no idea how she met her new supplier, Oz. He was tall, nice, friendly, and business-minded. Best of all, he kept his hands off me.

I was the youngest one, so my mom started using me to go to the washateria to pick up pounds of weed. After she got a better connection, she started having me ride the train to Odessa, Texas to pick up weed. I always left with a lot of money and came back with no money. They hid the weed a little better, just in case.

But Mom was always there to pick up me and the luggage. We went from the poor house to having everything a person could ever dream of having.

Without a car and her inability to drive, we always had a driver, or she hired cab drivers to assist me and her wherever we wanted to go. We had a maid and bodyguards. Several people worked for my mom. It got crazy at times. Before she started making lots of money from the drugs, we lived in four different apartments, but in the same complex. In the last apartment, people lined up around the corner to buy weed. I often wondered if someone planned a concert I didn't know about, and all those people waited to get front-row tickets. That's how it seemed to me. But no. They were there to see my mother.

She walked around with a 30/30 shotgun. We had easy access to pistols all over the place. And they were loaded, so we didn't play around with them. They weren't toys, and we knew it. We counted money for days after she scored a shipment. But she always had weed stashed away—pounds and pounds of it hidden in a secret compartment in the master bedroom ceiling. No one ever thought to look there.

She had a large safe, workers on the front door and in the back of the apartment. No one was gonna mess with any of us. Only she and I had access to my bedroom. For once, I had hope that the nasty stuff would end.

A literal mastermind at being a criminal, Mom cussed and fussed at anyone who didn't move as fast as she expected. And she had some pretty high expectations of the speed at which anyone should obey her commands. Everyone at The Riverside Village was either on her side or in her pocket. So if the cops ever tried to bust her there, they didn't get any cooperation. Not even they touched my mother. She was truly a shrewd businesswoman—even though her business was illegal. Mom totally ruled her little world. But it wasn't without danger.

One particular night, things got really wild. She and Oz had to go get more weed, which confused me. We had some weed already stashed. Angel and I stayed behind. Mom didn't always want us there when she made a purchase. Somehow, two guys got into the apartment. Both had guns. One stood with the barrel pointed in our direction, moving it between my sister and me. The other one grabbed me and stuck the gun to my head.

"Open the safe, little girl."

I shook my head hard.

"Open it. Or I'll kill you." A cold hardness glinted from his eyes. In spite of the calmness in his voice, I had no doubt he might pull the trigger.

Angel's voice shook. "Open it, Fern. Just open it."

"No."

"Please, baby. He'll kill you for sure. Open it."

"No! He might kill me, but if I open it up, Mom for sure will. I'll take my chances with this guy."

"You little b…" A loud noise came from outside.

"Mom's back!" Angel sounded relieved.

One of the guys cussed and then said, "We gotta split. She'll shoot us for sure." He grabbed a fairly large bag of weed from the coffee table and sprinted out the door.

The other one headed for the door but stopped before leaving. "You better be glad she came back when she did. Next time, you better open the safe, or I'll just blow you away."

Angel flew across the room, gathering me in her arms. "You should've told him. What if he killed you? I couldn't stand it if you weren't here."

Even with all her demons, my sister still wanted to protect me. I loved her for it, but I feared Mom's wrath more than anyone else. And she might have just killed both of us if I had opened the safe. For once, I got to protect my big sister instead of her protecting me.

After she kicked Angel out of the house, Mom moved me out of the apartments and into some Townhomes. Because of the incident at Riverside, she didn't want to keep taking me there. But it didn't stop her from selling drugs, nor protect me from the craziness that came with her trade.

One day, I left school and got ready to cross the street. We lived directly across from Morningside Middle School, which was one reason she picked the townhomes. One of the men I recognized as a business associate of Mom's approached me and tried to get me in a van. No way was I going with him. He wasn't one of the men who usually drove me. When he tried to force me inside, I screamed. He let go and ran.

I told Mom and watched the fury flash in her eyes. That was when she hired Mr. Garcia to drive me to school. It seemed a little ridiculous to get in a car to go across the street, but I sure didn't want to be kidnapped. Mr. Garcia didn't make it easier with his sexual advancements toward me. Every time he made a suggestion, black storm clouds rose up and poured out of me. But I never told Mom. My mind always drifted back to Angel. She told Mom Jay wanted to have sex with her. Mom responded by putting her out.

What if she put me out because Mr. Garcia kept asking me to have sex? Where would I go? I considered every relative we had. None of them seemed like a very good option. None of them ever treated me with kindness. So no matter how bad it felt, I kept the secret, fearing my mother wouldn't love me anymore, and I'd end up on the street or something worse. I shuddered thinking about the possibilities of how bad my life could get if she got mad and put me out. That wasn't gonna happen.

I sucked it up and let Mr. Garcia make his remarks. But I didn't let him take advantage of me. At least I figured out how to stop that from happening with him. Besides, I had nice clothes and other things. I didn't want to mess that up. I'd figure out a way to make life better.

Somehow it had to feel better.

Chapter 8

With no friends at school, misery became my best friend. A smart kid, I did well in school though. I played the clarinet and took ballet. At least for a while. The teachers all liked me, and for once, I found people who treated me well. The teachers were all nice to me. I wasn't sure why. Maybe they thought I was different—not in all kinds of trouble like a lot of the kids.

At the apartments after school, friends surrounded me. While I won't mention their names, they all know who they were. I could count on them.

Of course, once I started drinking MD 20/20 and Mickey's beer and smoking weed, things weren't so great. I didn't do well in school after that. But my friends didn't care. They still accepted me unconditionally. That was a new feeling. And most of them showed respect to my mother, which meant even more after I heard so many relatives badmouth her.

I'm not sure what happened, but the weed and money ran out. Oz kept coming around helping Mom, but then one day, he was just gone too. What now? We put our furniture in storage. The owners stole it, and all of the sudden we had no place to live. Homeless.

I didn't like it.

We moved in with a guy and his son. I didn't like the idea of it, but then again what could they do that hadn't already been done? I didn't expect anything worse than the possibility of another man who wanted to have sex with me. But one night it happened. Mom and I were there alone when two men broke in. One of them put a gun to my head.

Again? I acted bravely the last time someone had a gun pressed against my temple. But that time fear of my mother kept me from doing what they asked. On that night, though, terror sped through my veins. My heart pounded, my head wondering what they wanted from us.

"Take off your clothes and get in the bathtub," one of them directed.

At first, Mom resisted, but then she nodded at me. "Do what they say, baby."

We undressed and climbed into the tub, shivering as much from fear as from cold.

"Lay down and stay there."

We didn't argue. As they rummaged through the apartment, we heard drawers and doors opened. I imagined the mess they were leaving for us. But this time, I didn't care so much. Mom called the shots for the two of us, so I didn't have to worry about her killing me anyway.

But why did they have us undress? Did one or both of them plan on raping us? I hoped not. I'd had so much of that.

One of them stood guard at the bathroom doorway while the other one worked. He looked over both of our bodies, a hunger in his eyes I knew all too well.

Mom must've picked up on it. "If you're going to rape us, do us a favor and kill us too."

What? "No," I begged. "Please don't kill me. You can rape

me, but don't kill me."

I glanced over at my mother. A harshness glinted in her eyes. Her anger pulsated in the veins in her neck. I'd seen that anger with other people. Maybe I should let the guys kill me. She looked like she wanted to.

The other man returned. "Let's go." He turned to us. "Stay in that tub for a while, and don't call the cops. If you do, we'll come back and kill you both."

I believed him. At least I sure wasn't gonna test him.

They left, and Mom fumed for what seemed like hours. In reality, it wasn't that long, but she went on and on about how it would have been better to die than to be left after they raped us. She had no idea of all I already endured—often at the hands of people she trusted. I could endure rape, but I wasn't ready for my life to be over. Survival instinct took hold of me that night. I couldn't understand why she'd rather die than to live after rape. I'd been raped and molested so many times, it didn't matter anymore.

We didn't stay with that man for long but started living from motel to motel. While at a Travel Lodge, my sister and her boyfriend came to stay with us. She and Mom always fell asleep early, but her boyfriend didn't. He found it quite fun to throw the covers back and show me his naked body. I wasn't amused.

Mom got back in the drug business. I was in high school by that time. A ninth grader living in hotels with a mother known as Marijuana Mama Carolyn Sue. Everyone respected her. Everyone but the cops of course. They busted her for selling weed.

Perhaps to stay ahead of the cops, Mom wanted to have her fortune read. She had two resources she used—Mrs. England and Mr. Jorge. They both practiced witchcraft, and they were good at it. Eventually, they taught my mom some. She kept a black cat, candles and cards she learned to read very well. If something didn't go her way, she used the black magic. I personally hated visiting both of these people. I swore they were using black magic on Mom.

She didn't think so, though. And she kept visiting them. Of course, the magic didn't prevent her from an arrest. We ended up in a Days Inn, where the most terrible experience happened. One night, while I watched TV, Mom went out for a soda. She didn't come right back, but I wasn't too worried. Hours passed. At some point, I fell asleep.

The next morning, I woke up. Looking over at the other bed, relief washed over me. I didn't realize I really was a bit worried. She lay there, covered from head to toe. As I started moving around, Mom woke up. I stood there in horror when she finally poked out her head.

"Mom, what happened to all your beautiful hair?"

"Some jerk shaved off all my hair."

I looked at her eyes. She cut them down. "Did he hurt you?"

"No. Of course not."

"Are you sure?" She curled up, moving gingerly. "Did he rape you?"

"No. I'm fine. He just scared me. Let's get going."

I didn't believe her. She moved in a way that reminded me of the way I felt after being raped. Memories of the physical pain of being forced to have sex flooded my mind. I was pretty sure Mom fought hard to prevent it. I knew she'd rather die than live with having been raped. But she didn't die, and I was glad. Still, I think she probably wanted to hide the truth from me.

We landed at Motel 6, and I transferred to Eastern Hills and then to Dunbar High School. I didn't really care since I had no school friends anyway. We were broke—again. But I had every color of Polo shirt available. Snake shoes, mink coats, diamond rings—all the things that smelled like we had money. It wasn't obvious we were homeless. But several of the girls didn't like me. They called me names and tried to pick fights with me.

In tenth grade at that point, I became sexually active with many different guys. Perhaps that was why those girls didn't like me. The guys did though, and I didn't see any problem with it.

Of course, with no money, I had no more pre-arranged rides anywhere. I walked from the hotel to school every day. Then this white guy offered me a ride. I figured I could always jump out of his car, so although mistrust stuck to me, I accepted. He picked me up and dropped me off near the school, so the other kids had no idea I lived in the motel. They just saw me getting dropped off. I thought he was a really nice guy, but as always it went south one morning.

"How about you pay me for all these rides?"

"I ain't got no money. Do it look like I got money?"

"There are other ways." Uh-oh. That look. I hated that look. "I need some sex. It's been a while since I had any."

Ironic—I had so many guys at school, but I wasn't about to give anything to this older man in his car. Some things just aren't right. And a full-grown man with a young girl is one of those things. I didn't even bother replying. I opened the door, tucked and rolled. I never saw him again, and I wasn't sorry.

I kept walking to school and didn't tell anyone about the man—not even Mom. What difference did it make? He was gone, and for once the older guy didn't get what he wanted from me. That had to be something positive, right?

Chapter 9

Not all of life was terrible. I had good friends, like James and Jen. They cared about me. James' granddad owned the Motel 6. He knew we had only the clothes in bags and nowhere to live. He tried to help us. Jen asked her grandmother if we could live with them. Bless that woman—may she rest in peace. She agreed. Even now, I remember these people who at least tried to help us out. And I am forever grateful for them. Although life wasn't always good for me, those bright spots gave me hope for something better. How do you say thank you for something like that—something you can never repay?

None of that lasted long. We moved from one place to another during my ninth- and tenth-grade years in high school. Homeless. What a way to describe yourself so young in life. Mom started selling weed again, so other than lawyer fees, our situation started looking better.

Mom took me out of Dunbar and transferred me to Paschal. Mom was part of a prestigious charitable organization known for good works. She owned a daycare. But when she got busted, we ended up back on the south side of town.

By that time, I met a guy and started dating him, clueless

about his other girlfriend. Mom didn't keep her feelings about him a secret.

"What do you want to be with him for? I hate him."

"He's not so bad, Mom. Why don't you like him?"

"I just don't. I don't trust him. Besides, he ain't good enough to be with you."

"You don't think anyone's qualified to be with me."

"That's not true—just not anyone you've met so far. You're better than him—better than all these fools. You deserve the very best, and he sure ain't it."

"Oh, Mom." I shook my head. Obviously, she didn't know everything about me. I wasn't any better than anyone else. If she knew the truth…

Being sexually active was no big deal for me. So of course, this guy was no exception, and I ended up pregnant. I didn't know what to do. I knew how much my mother hated my boyfriend, and this probably wasn't gonna make it better.

One day I chatted with Mom's friend, trying to sound normal but with the thoughts of a baby weighing heavy on me.

"What's the matter with you, girl? Your mind's a million miles away from here."

"I'm pregnant, and I don't know how to tell my mom. She hates my boyfriend."

"Oh, girl. I know that's true. She talks smack about him all the time."

"She's gonna be so mad."

"Nah. Maybe at first, but she'll get over it. You want me to tell her for you?"

I should've known that was a bad idea. "Would you? Maybe you can soften her up a little."

"Sure, girl. It'll be fine."

But it wasn't fine. That night, Mom put a gun to my head. I

literally thought she intended to kill me.

"You're gonna have an abortion tomorrow."

What? I wasn't sure about being a mom, but I didn't really want to abort this baby either. I swallowed hard.

"And I ain't paying for it. That fool got you pregnant. He or his family need to take care of it."

The next morning she woke me up early and pushed me to the car. We went to my boyfriend's house and sat down with him and his mother.

"So what do you intend to do about this? You need to pay for the abortion."

His mother looked at me. "Is this what you want?"

I shrugged my shoulders. Did it matter?

"You don't have to get an abortion," she said. "I'll help you."

Sure she'd help me. I didn't believe her. No one much had ever helped me, and how could this woman protect me from my own mother? I looked over at Mom. She glared at me and shot daggers from her eyes toward the boy and his mother. I still wasn't sure Mom wouldn't kill me. I was pretty sure she had the gun with her and might use it on all three of us. I didn't want that on my conscience.

"It's okay. I'll do what my mom says."

We left and went straight to the abortion clinic.

There, so many emotions ravaged my mind. Why didn't Mom want me to have the baby? Even though she hated the dad, it was half me. I couldn't figure out her thinking. Confused, I accepted what came, the entire time overwhelmed by relentless loneliness. I feared the process and my mom—to this day not certain which scared me more. As I lay on the table, life drained from me, leaving me numb and empty.

Afterward, Mom took me to the Green Oaks Motel, for

what was the worst night of my life. I'd been through so many terrible nights, but none compared to that one. She had her gun and kept pointing it at my head, cocking it and staring at me as if she wanted to pull the trigger. It didn't take much for me to believe she was serious.

I couldn't control the rapid pace of my heart, so wild I thought it might burst and save her the trouble of shooting me. I finally called a friend, trying anything to calm myself. We talked very quietly until I fell asleep, still not certain if I'd wake up or be killed while I slept.

The next day we went back to the apartment. Shortly afterward mom bought me a car and gave me a curfew. I was already smoking weed and drinking MD 20/20 on a regular basis and had been since the age of 10. With all the bad in my life, it was the way I coped with things.

After a while, the pain started to lessen, but the racing thoughts got worse and worse. At that time, I had no idea what was going on with me. I continued to attend Paschal High School and got a job at Wendy's. But the day they asked me to wash the window Mom told me to quit. So that didn't last very long.

Mom kept me with so much money in my pocket and all the new clothes I could wear. Every day I had a new outfit and new purses and shoes. I rarely wore the same thing twice. I still had asthma too but not as bad as before.

One day, Mom had to run error. She asked me not to sell any weed while she was gone. But this guy showed up, looking for her. He seemed familiar, like one of her regulars, so I decided to sell it to him. He turned out to be an undercover agent.

The attorney told Mom if she pleaded guilty they would not lock me up. Considering I was in the 11th grade going to the

12th, she took the case and got me off. Mom, however, went to prison.

Chapter 10

How quickly life's journey can change. Mine certainly did.

From the time I hit fifth grade, my mom always sought out a reader who could predict the future and make bad things happen to people. One reader, Mr. Jorge, practice witchcraft and satanic rituals to the extreme. However, he gave me things to do to help my mom get out of jail. Each time they worked.

These people terrified me. After a while, Mom started reading cards, burning candles and using different potions. Many don't believe such darkness exists. It doesn't sound real, but I have seen satanic worship first hand. And I can attest it does really exist.

After one of the times when Mom got out of jail, she caught another case. This time she made the papers. Marijuana Mama Carolyn Sue, complete with photographs. Wow! It was horrible. She was no longer a part of her beloved prestigious organization and lost her daycare. You can't sell drugs when you have a bunch of innocent children under your care.

I looked for a job and quickly learned how to take care of myself. I started stealing—literally walking in and out of stores with large quantities of items, running credit cards, and writing checks. I worked at a jewelry store, but the paycheck wasn't enough to live on. Still, I figured out how to use that job to make a living. I stole jewelry from the store, then sold it to the drug dealers.

My mom wrote letters to me explaining how to sell drugs and who to score from. She put all the details in the letter. I would take it to the dealer, and he would front me the weed so I could deliver it as she requested. That didn't last long. And once again, I found myself without a place to live. This time, Mom wasn't around moving me from hotel to motel. But her friends, Janice and Jose, let me live with them.

Jose welcomed me. "You can stay here until your mom gets out of jail. But you can't tell anyone. I mean no one at all."

I was desperate to get Mom out of jail, even though I liked her friends. Jose introduced me to the world of cocaine, the first person who ever taught me how to cook it and free base. Oh my goodness, that was the best experience I ever had. My entire body left the earth. My mind was clear. My pain was gone, and all I wanted was another hit.

In trying to free my mother, I met a bail bondsman. He happened to be looking for Jose because he skipped bail. I had no way of knowing that, and without realizing what I was doing, I let it slip where he could find Jose. Of course, he got busted, and Janice kicked me out.

Where could a young girl go? I called my old boyfriend who fathered the child I aborted. His sister welcomed me to come live at their house. Then one night, she dropped a bomb on me.

"You know he has a baby with another girl."

"What?"

"Yeah. She was pregnant when you got pregnant."

I couldn't stay there any longer. With nowhere to go, I packed my few belongings and slept in my car. I wanted to die.

Life meant nothing. But I wasn't gonna kill myself, and I couldn't die. So I kept going to school and living in my car for the time being.

Then one day they called me to the principal's office. Someone told him I was minor living alone. He called one of my relatives and insisted she come to the school.

In his office, she said, "Of course, she can live with me. I had no idea she was living alone." She smiled at me. "C'mon sweetie. Let's go home."

As soon as we were outside of the school, she turned to me. "You can continue going to school, but you can't live with me. Sorry."

She made sure no one watched as we went our separate ways. I lived in an apartment until the money ran out, but the manager found out I was a minor and told me I couldn't live there alone. Out of money and with nowhere to go, I turned to what I knew best.

There was a man named Mel who at the time was the biggest drug dealer in the county. I went to see him, telling his guys up front that I needed money.

When they finally let me see him, he asked, "Why you coming to me asking for money, girl? I don't know you."

"You know my mom. She's in jail, and I'm in a bad situation."

"Okay. I know this couple. Take this ounce to them, and when you return I'll pay you." He was using their shop, and they were friends of my mom.

"If you stay in school, I'll let you work for me."

"Deal." I had no problem with staying in school.

Things started to look up, so I thought. I could work for Mel, stay in school and everything would be just fine. But one day I went to see him. The Feds were all over the place, one of them handcuffing him.

He pointed me out. "Can I talk to my young friend there, tell her what's going on?"

"Sure," they responded.

I ventured over to Mel.

"Do you know Dub?"

"No."

"Okay, good. Then don't ever go there."

After everything died down, I told my cousin, "Let's find Dub."

It didn't take us long to track him down at the Club Mac. A couple of guys who worked there realized I was living in my car. They took pity on me and allowed me to sleep in the back of the club as long as I stayed in school. I got up and got myself ready each morning. It was a simple way to have a place to live with no bad strings attached, but it wasn't easy. And my grades suffered. I started failing.

One of my counselors, Mrs. Major, took a great interest in me. I wasn't sure why, but I suppose she liked me and saw some potential in me. She got me involved in the Jabberwock Program, and I became a debutant. She remained diligent in me graduating high school, calling me every morning until she got a notice from the office saying I was in my first class. I went to school every day even if I was late because I promised my mom I would graduate.

By this time, I had the courage to tell my biological father Mom was in prison. His oldest daughter allowed me to come live with her for a while, but most of the time I lived in my car.

Apparently, Dub noticed every time he came to the club in the morning, I was there getting ready for school.

One morning he approached me. "Girl, how old are you?"

"16—almost 17." I wasn't sure how he'd react, but I didn't

want to lie to him.

"Where are your parents?"

"My dad's around, and my mom is in prison."

He shook his head. Next thing I knew, he helped me and my cousin get a place to live. We were in the time of our life with access to pounds of cocaine, unlimited access to all the money we could spend and freedom to drink as much alcohol as we wanted. Dub stated as long as I was 17, he would not touch me. And he kept his word. But the day I turned 18 ushered in one of the worst nights of my life. It seemed he kept all of his desire for me pent up until that night. Keep in mind, all of these men were old enough to be my dad or grandfather. Although I didn't have a problem giving myself away, I hated doing it with the old men.

I lived in different motels as much as I lived in the apartment. I started sleeping with most of the drug dealers in the community that could afford to give me whatever I wanted as well as send my mom money. They provided me with the resources to visit her as often as I could when I wasn't using.

Eventually, I met another drug dealer that basically had the city sewed up. He got me a different apartment and took care of me and my mom and sister who was also in prison. He never allowed me to sell drugs for him, but he did allow me to keep money for him. My drug addiction had gotten so bad I started doing everything under the sun. Nothing mattered more than my next score.

I finally met Tiny who was heavily involved in selling drugs. We used to smoke crack off a kilo over several weeks at a time. He would sit the kilo in the middle of the floor. We stayed up for days—sometimes weeks—with just a little sleep. I loved being with Tiny.

But I continued to see Dub and the other dealer at the

same time. It was easier for me to have all of my bases covered so I never ran out of drugs. I continued to steal even though I didn't have to. I enjoyed the thrill of stealing from stores and people, especially if they were watching me. I had a gift to talk and use my hands very quickly. I never got caught because of my demeanor. I always dressed nice, spoke in a vernacular people could understand and lived in an environment different from most drug addicts. The queen of wearing a mask, I could fool most anyone.

I was not a Christian—didn't even know God or much about Him. But every time I got high, I had to turn on Robert Tilton. When he prayed I laid my hands on the screen. I sat on the floor for hours looking at the carpet, then road around town for days in a daze. Drugs had me so spaced out, yet I would not stop smoking crack. During a visit, I told my mom if I ever did please make sure all my friends had pipes and crack as my casket was being lowered in the ground.

Next, I met an African man, Jim. He had a lot of money and drove a Mercedes. For some reason, he liked me a lot, giving me anything I wanted. Often I stayed gone for days, but he always let me back in the house. I lived a double life for a long time. In Dallas, I was a devout Muslim. In Fort Worth, I was a hustler.

Always highly skeptical of people, I never let others in my circle, nor did I get high with other people. Tiny and my friend, which I call my sister, were the two exceptions. And even that wasn't necessarily the best decision.

Tiny was very high one day and pushed me into the living room. He started burning me with cigarettes. I screamed because of the pain. A man knocked on the door and made Tiny let me out of the house. I went and found my dealer friend, but Tiny kept calling me.

"Come to my house, baby. I miss you. I won't hurt you."

"You don't want to go there," my friend said. He gave me half an ounce. "Here. Take this and go home."

"Okay." I took the drugs and went to my own place.

The next morning I got a text. "You with Tiny? I heard he got popped last night."

I stared at my phone in disbelief. I could've been with him. I could've died. And if I didn't want that to happen, something had to give.

Chapter 11

The lifestyle of drugs and all that went with it wore thin. And Tiny's death rattled me. Perhaps a change of scene?

I tried to escape drugs by moving to San Antonio with my cousin. But no sooner had we arrived than I met another drug dealer—Mario. That did not go well. This was a different part of my life.

When I arrived, we went to HEB. Without thinking, I sacked my groceries. The manager saw me and liked the way I put groceries in the bag. He hired me. It felt like a fresh start. Maybe someone finally would give me a legitimate break. I was living with my cousin and things looked better.

As I worked one day, I noticed a distinctive pin on a woman's lapel, and it triggered memories of Mom.

"My mom used to be in that organization," I commented.

"We don't have any niggers in our groups."

"Mom is not a nigger. Her name is Carol." I dismissed any offense and walked out to her car, pushing the cart with her groceries.

I didn't expect the question that came from nowhere. "Can you come to my house for lunch on your off day?"

"Sure."

Mrs. Eastern apparently liked me for some unknown reason. Maybe because of the potential connection between her and my mother. I told her I was trying to get an apartment where my cousin lived.

My family is the Wurzbach. We own most of the land on Wurzbach Street. What is the name of the apartments?"

After I answered, she said. "No problem. I'll help you out."

When I left her house that day, I called my cousin. "Guess what. I can move into an apartment for $14.00."

What amazing luck. But my old demons wouldn't leave me alone, and I started using again. I smoked every day, eventually losing my job. Out of money, I sold all my furniture to a neighbor and then called the police saying I was robbed. I ended up moving back to Fort Worth.

While I lived in San Antonio I met a lady that ask me to go to church with her. Each Sunday she and her husband picked me up. I was so out of it, I could not sit up in church. But Pastor Nice preached anyway. After service, she walked through the crowd. She came over to me, laid her hands on me and prayed. One lesson that seeped in during that time was the importance of paying tithes. I'm not sure why that stuck with me.

I didn't believe in God, but I did believe in me. So I thought I was god. Memories from childhood surfaced during that time. When I was a kid, I went to Love and Care Nursery. The owner used to take me to Mount Rose Church, and I listened to the choir sing. One lady sang "I am going up yonder." I remembered that song through my entire addiction.

I blamed my disbelief of God on Jay. When he was molesting me, I used to tell him God was going to get him.

His words still haunt me. "If God was real, could I do

whatever I want to do to you?"

At that point, I knew he had to be right. God couldn't be real, could he? I excluded God from my life, and it continued even while I sat in church listening to the pastor preach.

As I was in my addiction, I met a man named Kurt, also a drug dealer. He came to my house, and we spent all night smoking crack. He always brought so much crack I couldn't sleep or eat. The entire time I used, I never experienced a moment when I dreamed drugs would ever be a problem for me. I never imagined stopping.

Afterward I stopped seeing everyone but Kurt and one other drug dealer. Most of that was because the head of all of them got busted. They all received sentences of 25 to life in prison. Even then, I didn't worry. I always seemed to have a good connection to all the drugs I wanted.

I made a new friend, and the two of us started stealing cars for a living, selling them to the Cubans. By this time, they had taken over the presidency in the drug game. They made it easy for me to stay supplied.

Then I met a guy who went by Street. He was pretty much the leader, and he really liked me. Street provided me with all the drugs and fun I wanted. He made sure no one else took advantage of me. I didn't have that all the time, even when I was with Tiny. But after Tiny's death, I was able to move freely in the different circle. Somehow I always knew who to connect with. I set my sights on the man with the most money, the nicest car, and the best drugs.

I also met a man named Randy that had a different kind of hustle. He moved all kinds of merchandise and money. Although he never introduced me to his game, he made sure I kept more than enough money in my pockets. Most guys brought dark trash bags full of money to my house. The goal was for me to keep it safe, and I could spend as much as I wanted as long as they left the drugs. It wasn't really necessary for me to leave my apartment.

To a young girl without any parents or loving family around, it was a dream life. I went from experiencing homelessness to living like a queen. And the drugs helped me cope with any part of it I didn't particularly enjoy. Besides, I always had my closet mind if I needed to escape. As time went on, I became so accustomed to my lifestyle I didn't need to escape mentally. The drugs became my closet without my realizing it.

After Mom got out of prison she had everything she needed. Only one thing was different—she no longer wanted to be a drug dealer or be involved with them. But we still got high together. Either I gave her drugs, or we bought them for one another. A weird relationship between a mother and daughter, but to us it was normal. Every man I associated with knew if he wanted to be in my life, he had to take care of my mother and niece. There was no other way to be in my life. Most of them had no issue with my terms.

After most of my friends got busted, life became a hard pill to swallow. Forced into it, I ventured into avenues I hadn't experienced before, such as low-life prostitution. I was never on the streets, but I was with guys for $100.00. I grew accustomed to trash bags full of money in my possession and the freedom to spend it. Even if I turned a trick every day, I didn't have that kind of money. And drugs cost money, so one a day wasn't necessarily enough. Any man was a possibility at that point. I started to lose my dignity and integrity.

At some point, I partnered with my best friend who was a dancer. We went to Lawton, Oklahoma where she convinced me to start dancing. I was not a good dancer because I have no rhythm. However, I was very provocative, so most men tipped me well. I hated dancing—my dignity plummeted to a new low.

I used more drugs and added Budweiser and tequila to dance. Every night I got high enough to go out on stage, and even then I felt every eye bore into me. So many men watching, their tongues practically hanging out and drool easing down their chins. I didn't have to guess what their minds imagined. I remembered the look from all the people who molested me. Dancing topped my experiences as one of the most horrible.

I met this guy and got pregnant, but he led me along. Many empty promises of being together and him taking care of me.

One day a girl told me where he lived, so I went and knocked on the door. A lady answered and called him to the door.

He stared at me coolly with the woman standing beside him. "I don't know her. Never seen her in my life. She looks like some cracked-out whore."

I needed him to own up to his responsibilities, but I knew he wouldn't. All the promises floated over me and dissipated into the air—as empty as my heart felt.

I continued to use until I couldn't stand up. One day, Mom asked me to take my niece to the ER. She was really sick.

The doctor examined her and then turned to me.

"You look pretty far along. Can I check you?"

I shrugged. Why not? I hadn't seen a doctor, even being pregnant.

He did an exam and said, "Your water broke—I'm guessing about five days ago."

"What? I had no idea. I never had a kid before."

He just shook his head. "We need to induce labor now."

He immediately induced labor. I gave birth to a little boy, but when he came out, there wasn't a single cry.

Although I never had a baby before, I knew that wasn't right. "Why isn't he crying?"

The doctor answered in a flat tone. "He died. Probably soon after your water broke—maybe before."

Depression descended on me. I had at least five abortions, and then I added the miscarriage of a child. For some reason, his death hit me harder than any of the abortions. I was so disappointed in myself. I should've been more careful not to get pregnant or at least take better care of myself. Maybe he would have lived. It was all my fault.

The pain in my heart overwhelmed me. I couldn't think straight—not for a moment. So I did what I always did, turning to drugs again. Just a moment of relief or clarity. That's all I wanted. When I was high, I didn't care—I didn't think. Every time I stopped using, the pain got greater and greater.

After the doctor released me from the hospital and I recovered, I went back to work.

Dancing became a way of life—an avenue of survival. I hated every day and every minute.

Each morning I woke up and said, "I hate that I'm alive." I screamed, "Just let me die."

But I kept right on living—waking up to a new day that felt exactly like the one I lived the day before.

Driving one day, I was so high. I stopped the car on the railroad tracks. The horn blared, a huge hunk of steel bearing down on me. Brakes screeched against the rails as the massive engine tried to slow down. But you can't stop a fast-moving train without a lot of room. It hit me so hard you could literally see in the car.

I shouldn't have survived, but I did. How? And why? I wanted to die. After an attempt sure to succeed in death, I still lived.

The conductor jumped out and tried to retain me. He begged me to stay put. For all he knew, my car died on the tracks, and I couldn't get out. I didn't admit the whole thing was intended to end my life. I pulled away from him and made my way to a drug house.

It was too much to bear.

Chapter 12

I was one of those people that did not have a heart or conscience. I had a warped primary goal in life. Live to be used and live to use. I wanted to hurt every person I met. If I could get you, I was happy—even happier if I got you before or without you getting me. I did not like or trust anyone, extremely paranoid of all people.

For many periods of life, Mom and I shared drugs and got high together. Yet, we didn't have a good relationship. We fought all the time and cussed at each other like we were from the streets.

In the back of my mind, I thought she knew of every man that molested me and every person that hurt me. How could she be a mother and not know all those things? I kept trying to figure out why she never helped me. Why didn't she stop it? I always fell asleep, blacked out or disengaged from my body, leaving my mind. By the time she came home, I was awake, so I believed she never left home. In my mind, she was responsible for all the bad things that happened to me. A mother is supposed to protect you, and she didn't. I couldn't rectify it all in my head. Yet I didn't talk to her about the bad things I experienced. She just had to know, and in my messed up state of mind, it made me detest her. How was I supposed to deal with this strange love-hate relationship?

I moved back and forth from Dallas to Fort Worth regularly.

When mom went to prison the second time I was in the 11th grade. I had to learn how to take care of myself. Ironically, the largest drug dealer at the time helped me get on my feet. Even then, I went from drug dealer to drug dealer.

I was raped at gunpoint. My drug usage became so bad I was smoking off a kilo every day for several weeks at a time. I weighed about 90 pounds. I stole jewelry from a store where I worked and drew a decent paycheck. That wasn't enough, so I stole cars and sold them for a living. After that, I stole clothes by the boxes from different clothing stores.

I have slept with over 100 men and have had 10 abortions.

Not a resume that I take pride in at all. That was my life, and at the time, it all seemed completely normal. Wasn't that how everyone lived? Everyone I knew lived pretty much the same way I did.

At one point, I moved in with Jim in Dallas. We opened a dry-cleaner store, clothing store and tape store. Legitimate businesses without all the drug dealers hanging around. We made so much money it was crazy. But I could not stop using, so I made my way back to Ft. Worth as often as I could without Jim really knowing what was going on. I robbed him every chance I got because he was very careless. Realistically, he trusted me. Then again, he didn't know I was on drugs. I somehow managed to hide that fact from him. He just knew I took off in a split second and stayed gone days at a time.

One day, my mom told me she had a friend for me to meet. I had no idea who he was. All I knew is he had plenty of money and lots of drugs, so that was my "Q" from her that I needed to meet him. After several attempts, she finally convinced me.

We all met at his house. Clifford was 61, and I was 25. He had talked me into going to a club with him. To my surprise, he didn't try to have sex with me that night, but he did give me a bag of crack cocaine and $400.00. I woke up a couple of days later and ran to Jim's house. By this time he was so tired of me, he locked me out. I went back to Fort Worth. Clifford was interested, so he let me stay at his house for a while.

One day, I was on my way back to Dallas. The police pulled me over because I was smoking crack in the car. He took me to jail for outstanding warrants. Oh my goodness. Shocked at the news, I found out the Feds had a warrant for my arrest.

Before I met Clifford, I had gotten involved with this younger guy. He and his dad were drug dealers, but they owned a detail shop. I had introduced the old man to my sister, so she started selling drugs for him. I was working at a Country Club at the time, which is where I met this guy. He convinced me to go out of the country with him. I did. Old habits don't go away when you leave the country. Needless to say, I ended up stealing some jewelry and was sent to prison in a foreign country. Mom sought out help to get me back home. Even before that, we were still stealing cars and selling them to the Cubans.

So, I ended up with this older guy. Of course, under arrest and with a federal warrant out, I needed help. Jim would not accept any of my calls, but Clifford did. He sent me money, paid my attorney fees and made sure my mom was taken care of.

After a while, we found out the FBI wanted me for selling drugs to an undercover agent. I went to Federal Prison. Shortly after, my sister came to the same Federal holding jail. I pled not guilty, but a friend told me to change my plea. The sentence hanging over me consisted of a drug charge, and it carried up to 40 years if I was found guilty. This friend and my sister explained to me that as a first-time offender if I plead guilty, I would get a lesser charge.

I was not a believer in God, but my friend's grandmother was a preacher. I cried all the time, so my friend asked her grandmother to pray for me. She prayed with me every day and gave me scriptures to read. I diligently read them. One night I asked God to forgive me.

"God, if you get me out of this prison, I will give you my first-born son." I read the story of Hannah and Samuel, so I figured maybe it would work for me.

However, I did 15 months in prison. Just because God heard Hannah didn't mean he would respond to me the same way. Perhaps my motivation was a wee bit warped, but then again, I tried.

Another friend of mine gave my mom an apartment to live in and helped her get Section 8 housing, so my two nieces and she were safe. That was one of my concerns. I was sentenced to Alderson West Virginia. The US Marshalls, Michelle and Walter, asked the judge if they could fly with me. They knew I didn't know my sister was not in the same prison.

But they knew. And they told me a few things during the trip. One stands out. Take all my negative energy and do something positive.

Michelle told me, "You're a consumer, not a distributor. You have a drug problem. This is why you keep doing all the things you're doing."

I didn't believe her. I didn't have a problem with drugs. I liked using them. They were my escape, and besides, everyone I knew used them. (This was in 1989.)

I spent my 15 months in prison. I didn't do anything

constructive or make any new friends. I spent my days talking on the phone to Clifford and to Wilford, who was kind enough to give me a job at his alternator shop before I was sent to prison.

Clifford was nice enough to offer me a place to live when I got out. So after I was released, Wilford offered me my old job back, but I chose Clifford. He wasn't going to make me work, and besides, he was very nice to me. He gave me anything I wanted. He hated most that I smoked crack cocaine.

When I was in jail, I thought about so many things. My mind constantly raced with fear and loneliness. I lived in horror and discouragement, completely confused by life. I had no idea how to put things in place.

Over my entire lifespan, I always had a plan from A to Z. I always looked for a way to gravitate to something very evil, and I always had a hustle. For some reason, I could talk people into anything and talk myself out of everything.

On one occasion before I went to prison, I walked to a club called the 150. This guy asked me if I wanted a ride. I said yes. On the way there, he pulled out a knife, and I jumped out of the car going about 35 mph.

Amazing that someone I knew and his friend were on the same road right behind me. At the same time, the police were coming up the other side of the road and saw me bail. The police officer stayed with me and took me to JPS. My friend chased the guy, but they lost him.

Once I was speeding down the road and ran a stop light, creating a horrible wreck. I was so drunk the officer allowed me to be taken to JPS, and they concluded I was fine but needed a ride home. They simply let me go.

In several instances, I was so drunk I didn't know who I was or where I was at the time. I woke up naked, drunk and vomiting on myself. I engaged in wild fights, getting kicked out of clubs. No one wanted to be around me because either I was too high or too drunk. I never understood why I drank so much. I never liked the way alcohol tasted or smelled. Whenever I drank, I felt very drowsy but then became belligerent, angry and aggressive. After drinking I felt irritated, lonely, tired, frustrated and unable to remember what happened the day or night before.

Yet in spite of all that, I never realized I had a drinking problem until years later.

Drugs seemed to be the only thing that kept me calm. Thoughts and emotions raced through me—anxiety, fear, doubt, and pain.

I re-lived Jay molesting me so much. Any time I saw something spilled on the floor I got angry. (I still experience intense anger today when I see something spilled.) My mind floats involuntarily back to this man dropping semen on the floor as he went to the bathroom. Over the years, this played in my head like a tape recorder. I could still smell his body odor and feel his tongue between my legs.

I could never explain to anyone what was going on with me, not even after seeing several therapists. Being molested hindered me in so many ways. It caused me not to be able to focus, take care of myself, my kids or even hold a job. I could not have a specific plant in my house. For years, I never allowed anyone to buy me flowers or give me plants. I always asked them not to, or I threw them away because it reminded me of Jay.

I believe it hurt the most because he was my stepfather. He was the first man to treat me like his daughter. He bought me all kinds of gifts, and I equated that with love. When he violated me in such a fashion, he hurt me deeply—far beyond the physical pain and trauma. I was very disappointed in him—and in myself for not telling anyone.

Another thing that hurt me stemmed from having sexual identity problems. When I was in the second grade, my friend and I started to have sex with each other. We continued until we were older. Discussing it over the years, we realized we both were being molested by different people. That distorted our childhood and abilities to make sound decisions.

Being molested is horrible. There's no other way to describe it.

Over the years, I was in so many relationships, often with multiple men at the same the time. I allowed so many men to abuse me with all kinds of things—toys, other women, behaviors that are not even conducive to discuss.

With these kinds of problems, I started watching pornography when I was alone. I would spend a few minutes masturbating then asking myself, "Why am I doing this?"

I knew it didn't make me feel good, and I didn't want to do it. I knew there was a problem with masturbating, because I started with movies, used bananas, sticks, my hand and towels. I had no idea how to stop the urges, which overwhelmed me.

All of these things constantly worked through my brain during my time in jail, when I had little to do but think. After all of these men left my life, I still had to deal with me. I never faced myself. I just continued to use drugs—my own personal little closet for my mind.

Chapter 13

As a requirement after prison, I lived in a halfway house for a while. Clifford brought Mom to visit me. I caught a dirty UA in the halfway house, but the judge decided not to send me back to prison.

I went back to live with Clifford. He supplied me with nice clothes, a place to live and a child. Yes, I was pregnant by a 63-year-old man.

First, let me say, I did love him as much as I knew how to love a man. He was as good to me as he could be, along with his family. But during our relationship, he had a lot of women.

At the beginning of my pregnancy, he did not want me to have a crack baby. So he went to my PO, Randy from Federal Correction Institution, and told him I was using. One day I came out of the bathroom, where I'd been hiding out and smoking crack. My PO was sitting on the couch with Clifford.

Randy was the best. However, at that time, I hated him—especially that day.

He took one look at me. "I need you to take a UA. I know you're using."

I looked down at my feet. Busted.

"Fern, I really don't want to send you back to prison. I want to help you. But you gotta want that."

"I do." And I meant it. I didn't want to be in trouble.

Randy went to the judge, who said if I stayed clean, he would not send me back to FCI. Nevertheless, I accumulated over 20 dirty UA in 30 days. So Randy stepped up again and this time asked the judge to send me to Help is Possible.

Really? You aren't putting me back in prison? I was sentenced to nine months in the rehabilitation center. It somehow felt like prison.

I went to HIP and Lue would not allow me to leave. I cussed everyone out every day. I threatened to leave. I refused participation in group therapy sessions.

Every day for about seven months, I did this same routine. Clifford came and visited me, but that didn't help much. I didn't want to be there, and I blamed him. Yet I still needed him and wanted to see him. The confusion of mixed emotions running through me fit right in with my normal state of mind.

While there, one day, I started crying. The tears started slowly and then poured. I couldn't stop them, no matter how hard I tried to fight them back. Silent tears transformed into soft sobs, which slowly became torrents of wails.

I was so broken the entire center was shocked. They called Lue.

"What's wrong?" she asked me

I couldn't respond with anything other than more sobs.

Kelly was my main counselor. He was so helpful and wanted to see me successful.

I knew a lot of fear in my lifetime but never like that day. I was having a baby, with no place to live, no money, and no car. Clifford was getting ready to go to prison. He caught a case and had to turn himself in.

I still had a few connections—some of Jim's old friends. They let me sell boot-leg tapes and helped me get an old 1973 Maverick. So, I would be able to get around.

Lue helped me get an apartment and furnished it with everything Corey and I needed—from food and clothes to furniture.

I was most amazed that all the ladies in the place helped me name Corey. One night we were up late.

Hazel said, "Fern what are you going to name the baby?"

"I don't know. Maybe I'll name him after his dad."

Ronni and Precious started calling out names.

Precious said "Corey."

"What does it mean?"

No one seemed to know the meaning, but we all said, "Yes. His name is Corey Rashaad."

I chose his middle name, trying to be Muslim like my friend, who stood by me even in the roughest times.

Lue didn't stop there. She helped me better understand how to be a parent, start recovery and be more responsible.

The road turned for me, or so I thought. Clifford went off to prison, and his son decided I didn't need to live in his house. But I had a fully-furnished apartment. Clifford's oldest daughter offered me a job, but I was selling tapes, so I was ok.

And then the demon returned. I started using again, lost my apartment in Dallas and moved back to Fort Worth.

Chapter 14

When I moved back to Fort Worth, I moved in with my mom, using so much crack it was horrible. At that point, I weighed about 100 pounds.

I started to work at a burger place, so I was able to steal money there and sell tapes. I saw absolutely nothing wrong with my lifestyle. In my mind, using drugs wasn't a problem, and I wasn't hurting anyone.

I stole all of Corey's clothes, so I kept him sharp. I just didn't have to sleep around anymore, and that made me very happy. I was tired, and I sure didn't want any men around my son. I wasn't about to let him experience the things I went through as a very young child.

When Corey was a baby I had no clue about how to hold an infant, take care of or nurture a child. One day he lay in his swing, content. I was talking to myself and all of the sudden noticed he had muscles. When I picked him up, his tiny heart beat against his chest. I never realized that before.

I hugged him close to my chest, feeling life pour through his little body. For the first time in my life, there was another human being I could love—really love. And he could love me without any strings attached. What a concept! Pure, unconditional love. Real love, not the messed up version I always knew.

A strange desire rose up in me. I knew at that moment I wanted to make him proud of me, and I would give him the world.

I tried with all my heart. By the time Corey was a year old, Mom was no longer in the drug game. So she was not in agreement with my lifestyle as a person or parent. I continued stealing and using drugs. Of course, Corey's father was in prison, and with nowhere else to go, I lived with my mom. I used drugs every day.

I secured a tab at the local grocery store with the guy who owned the store. He knew I would hustle at night, so he always gave me what I wanted. After a while, he decided my tab was too high. He refused to give me credit until I paid him. So, I went to another store, but this guy would not give me credit either.

Mom told me to go to the local church. I refused. I still didn't believe in God, and I sure didn't want anything to do with a church. However, there was another guy who visited me every Saturday morning. No matter how high I was, he would tell me about Jesus. I sat and listened to him because I felt sorry for him. No one else in the apartment complex opened their door for him.

One day he came. I had just woken up. I was ready to listen to him, which I did. But I wasn't convinced he was telling me the truth about this Jesus. In my mind, Jesus was the white man King James wrote about to get black people's money. And what did He ever do for me? Where was this Jesus when all the bad stuff happened to me?

My mom finally convinced me to go to the church. Out of

options, I went and told the preacher I needed milk.

"What kind of milk do you need?" he asked.

"Whole."

"We don't have any here, but if you leave your address, I'll have my associate pastor bring some over to you."

What kind of deal was this? I figured he had some game to play, but Corey needed milk, so I gave him our address.

I headed down the street to meet some guy and met the preacher coming up the stairs.

He introduced himself.

"I'm heading out. Just give the milk to my mother. She's there with my baby."

He looked deep in my eyes. "No. Wait a minute. I have something to tell you. God wants me to talk to you."

I wasn't having any of that. "No way." I continued to walk off.

The preacher followed me. "Fern, please come back. Just give me a few minutes."

"No."

As I approached my guy's house, shots reverberated through the air. A man bolted from the guy's door, jumped into a waiting car and took off. I peeked inside, saw the guy lying in a pool of blood. I didn't go in—nothing I could do for him. And I sure didn't want to get caught up in a murder.

I turned around and went back toward the preacher. I might as well make sure I had a solid alibi, and a preacher seemed like a pretty good one. We walked back to my home.

Mom welcomed in the preacher and thanked him for the milk.

He turned to her. "I believe God wants me to pray for your daughter."

"She's a fool. She won't listen to you."

But the preacher took my hand and prayed. What difference did it make? It was just some words—a small price to pay for a gallon of milk.

A few days later, I took my clothes down to the laundry room. These kids talked about a church event on Friday nights called the Upper Room.

"What's that?" I asked.

They told me what little they knew. Their mom used to get high with me, so I asked if I could take the kids to church. She said yes. We went. I listened to the choir, and the kids had fun. As we were leaving, I met the pastor and his friends. Nice enough, but nothing life-changing.

I kept smoking crack, even though I wanted to stop for Corey's sake. But no matter how hard I tried to stop I could not. All I could think about was being molested, raped, hurt and abandoned. Confusion covered me like an old blanket—thin and worn, yet always there. I had no idea I suffered from depression and had mental problems. I never told anyone I could see things walking or hear voices. I thought it was the drugs, so I kept it to myself. I fought, cussed and went off at any given point. I continued these behaviors for several years, while life got worse. I didn't know how to make it better, and even though I kept trying to change, I couldn't. Eventually, everything turned so bad I wasn't sure I could stand it anymore.

Finally, I went back to the church. "Pastor, can I talk to you?"

"Of course you can."

"There was a pastor I met. He told me if I had sex with him on the pulpit, I would be saved. That was back in the late 1980s, and I slept with him at his church." I thought back to that incident. Jay told me God wasn't real, and that preacher confirmed it for me. I felt so bad about having sex in a church.

Why would God allow that preacher to make me feel so bad? "Pastor, I didn't feel saved. I felt bad about what happened."

Pastor sat for a minute. Tears filled his eyes and pushed over the side. "That preacher was a sick man. He shouldn't have done that. I will never hurt you. I'll never do something like that to you."

He was nice and friendly. That day he also told me about Jesus. I listened, but I did not believe him.

It wasn't until Associate Pastor Franklin explained to me about salvation that I truly believed God could save me. That day in 1994, I accepted Jesus as my personal Lord and Savior. But even then, I didn't stop using drugs.

My mom was so tired of me, she put me out in the rain. She called the police, and they took Corey and me to the Salvation Army. They were full that night, so we ended up at the Presbyterian Night Shelter. I'd been through some awful times, but this was the worst experience. I'd been homeless, but never in a homeless shelter, and it wasn't just me this time. I put all of our clothes under the cot, and we slept on the bed together.

How could life get any worse?

Chapter 15

The next day a lady told me about the women and children's program at Salvation Army. We went, and the next day they accepted us into the program. From there, they introduced us to YWCA daycare and many other programs. Maybe with help, life could get better.

Corey was a very sweet kid, and he always smiled. Everyone loved him. I tried so hard to stay off drugs, more for his sake than my own.

We were offered an apartment in the Peppertree. It wasn't my first time on my own. Mom going to prison left me alone at such a young age, but by then I had Corey. So things needed to be different. I managed to stay clean for a long time. I went to church regularly, paying my tithes and offerings, and trying to live right.

But some things didn't change. I continued to steal and sleep with different men, although I didn't let anyone around Corey. Whenever I had a date, I took him to my mom's. She welcomed having him, even overnight. I had two goals in mind—hurt as many people as I could and get as much money as I could.

I thought I enjoyed sleeping with all those men. But after one left I fell back into depression. Every day I took so many baths, even if I did not sleep with anyone. I always felt dirty.

So many thoughts drifted in and out of my mind, and ideas of killing myself popped up frequently. But I didn't want to leave Corey in foster homes. He was my lifeline. I wanted so badly to be a good parent. I bought him everything a child could want.

Living in the Peppertree was a totally new experience. We did not have any furniture downstairs and only a bed upstairs. The church I attended tried to give me furniture, but I refused it. I planned on a big income tax refund, and then I could buy all the stuff I wanted for us new. Clean and sober, working at a job and taking care of Corey, one big fear remained. Someday, his father would get out of prison. I knew if he did, I would have to be with him. I still loved him. But with him, I would use again. Even though he hated seeing me use, he preferred giving it to me rather than to see me doing anything wrong. Those thoughts haunted me. I continued to work and yes, Clifford got out of prison.

I was not excited, because I was afraid of me.

Knowing I was addicted to crack, he sold it for a living. And I continued to use. The irony of it all. Corey's father was a drug dealer, but he was totally against me using drugs. Nevertheless, he gave it to me. All the time he said he didn't want to, but he didn't want me out in the streets or doing anything else illegal to get drugs.

After he got out of prison he visited Corey, and he kept him until the day he passed away. May he rest in peace.

I really tried to escape using by going to meetings and church. For a while, I did well, but then I started back using again. The years of struggle pressed down on me, creating a weariness I couldn't end. I desperately wanted a way out.

One day, I met my second son's father. Huge mistake, although I didn't see it at the time. He didn't use drugs, and he helped me out a lot. We got engaged. Preparing to get married, he told me he had been common-law married for a while and had three children.

I knew about the children, but I really believed him when he told me he was separated. He had a good job and was really nice to Corey and me. I found my prince charming. And he wanted to take me away from the awful life I lived. He was not verbally abusive and never gave me drugs. I needed a man like that.

The day he told me he was married, I told him we could not see each other anymore. He agreed. An event during this time truly amazed me. I had repented and one day was praying. The Holy Spirit kept ministering to me and kept saying, "You will name him Isaiah." So I started reading the book of Isaiah in the Bible.

Shortly afterward I found out I was pregnant. I didn't hesitate to call his father, unsure whether it would change things between us.

His answer shocked me. "You should abort the baby."

After having had Corey, an abortion simply wasn't an option for me.

I held back the tears and did my best to keep my voice steady. "It's a boy, and his name will be Isaiah." At that moment, I decided to have Isaiah, with or without his father in the picture.

He asked, "How do you know it's a boy and why Isaiah? Are you that far along?"

"No, not at all. But I've been praying and listening."

I then told him what the Lord had ministered to me. He

didn't say much in response. However, he chose to stop seeing me or having any line of communication with me. He started leaving money on my door in envelopes, and he called, telling me to open the door. Even before I opened the door, he drove away.

After going through so much trauma as I child, I don't know if I ever experienced as much pain, hurt, betrayal and rejection. I felt so alone and unworthy. The pain gripped me more and more each day. I spent hours crying because yet another man left me. I spent days in depression. So many of those days I WANTED to kill myself, but I could not leave Corey alone.

The old demon reared its head, and I started smoking more crack. I put foil, sheets and blankets on the windows of my room and stopped taking care of myself and Corey. I have no idea how he made it through that time with good grades. He managed to stay a very strong, smart kid. He fed himself, washed his clothes and got the check from the mailbox, taking it to the local store where he cashed it to pay the bills and buy groceries. All of that as a second-grade kid. He was very smart but forced to learn how to do everything because I could not function.

How was I supposed to tell someone the depth of my pain or that I was having mental problems and drug problems? I managed to go to church and sometimes NA. For a while, I kept temporary jobs to make ends meet, but before long I quit. Misery became my constant companion. Making regular doctor appointments, I called Isaiah's father multiple times. He refused to talk to me or respond to calls or emails.

His extreme distance caused more depression. How could this man who supposedly loved me enough to propose simply ignore me when I needed him so much? Corey's father did his best to help me, even trying to get me off drugs. Not this man. He seemed not to care about me or his baby.

As expected, Isaiah arrived. What happened next took me completely by surprise. His father called CPS, and they removed Isaiah from the home, leaving me with a summons to appear in court. They offered only weekend visitation and Wednesday evenings. Anger bubbled up inside of me and spilled all over. Where was this man during Isaiah's birth? How dare he take me to court? Then the judge asked me to start visiting Isaiah only on weekends. Before long it went to every other weekend. After that, the judge limited me to one day, then only seeing him four hours and finally down to a single hour at a time.

I visited my baby for one hour for a very long time. Seeing my son for such limited time, yet with his brothers, filled my heart with more pain than I can describe, especially knowing his father originally wanted to abort him. Each time, my heart shattered a little more.

I asked God to bless me with another son. He did with Trenton. During this time, I didn't actively attempt suicide, but I kept trying to kill myself. I smoked crack for days until I passed out, always while Corey slept. When he came home from school, he found me still sleeping.

Foil, black trash bags, sheets or blankets covered the windows. Although I fed Corey, I didn't eat. I only visited Isaiah at the scheduled visitation.

By the time I conceived Trenton, I weighed about 98 pounds, continuing with crack during my entire pregnancy. I stayed at home until it was time to deliver, not really wanting to see the doctor. Because of Isaiah and my crack usage, CPS was called. We had to live with my mom until they closed my case.

They assigned me to a therapist, one who wasn't easily fooled. She realized there was something going on with me. I drove a very nice car, had a more than decent place to live, and CPS stated they could not label me as an addict. However, she walked me through the molestation abuse. Looking back at the abuse proved one of the most difficult things I ever experienced, but we worked on it weekly.

Being molested held me captive for so many years.

Although I didn't remain sexually active with humans, I was overly active with myself—a fact I never shared with my therapist.

The pain from Isaiah's dad hurt me worse than anyone. I didn't understand how he wanted me to have an abortion, but then he turned around and took me to court. He took my son away, and I had to pay child support. For several years I held resentment against him—until I realized he was looking out for the best interest of our son. In captivity, I couldn't handle the rejection of this man I loved. So I returned to the only way I knew to escape pain. The closet of my mind no longer existed, but drugs did.

Trenton was a cute baby. I really didn't realize I was pregnant until he was born, fully in denial that it was actually happening again.

With Trenton came another round of rejection. His dad had a girlfriend, and he wasn't willing to leave her for me. I was just a side note for him. He didn't meet Trenton until he was 5 years old, denying that Trenton was his son. Nevertheless, Trenton's paternal grandmother always acknowledged and kept him until she passed away. Surprisingly, Trenton always had the support of his dad's family. One of his cousins and his brother actually named my baby.

During this season of life, I met several people who tried to help me mentally, emotionally, financially and spiritually. God sent so many people, but fear, pain, hurt, rejection, abandonment and hate consumed me. My mind was not able to grasp the concept that God was real, nor that people really cared about and could help me.

Through all of these years, though, God never left me. He took me through a long process, developing me into the person I am today. Even at the lowest times, He worked in my heart, knowing He had a greater plan for my life than I ever imagined.

Chapter 16

While some people come into this world and follow an easy path for most of their life, some of us require a long journey—a process to take us down the path where God intended us to travel all along. Some of my early journey didn't match what anyone thinks of as a good plan. How could God allow such evil against a precious little girl?

Perhaps He knew someday I would overcome all of the trauma, stronger and able to help others break free from the captivity of their past. But getting me to that point from where I was didn't happen overnight. It required years of development.

The transformation process started in 1989. While in federal prison, I said a prayer I did not know God actually heard. "God if you get me out of this prison, I will give you my first-born son."

Around 2000, I started working at a cable company where I met Isaiah's dad.

I was home taking a break one day and clearly heard footsteps on my stairs.

I sat up and asked, "Who is it?"

A tender, yet strong voice answered me. "Fern, Fern,

Fern."

My hands trembled. "Yes?"

"Do you remember when you said you would give me your first-born son?"

How do you respond when you aren't living right, but you have no doubt God is speaking directly to your mind? "Yes." I must have sounded quite timid to anyone around, including Him. But I wasn't about to deny the promise. From that point, several events took place.

I was still using drugs off and on, yet working as much as I could. I went to church, but I was not 100% in the church. I still had a few men that helped pay my bills, robbing and stealing whatever I could to make ends meet instead of trusting God.

One day while having sex with a girl, we were fully engaged when I heard a voice. "You are changed."

Talk about a mood killer. I pushed her up and never went back to a woman.

I called the church and got involved in serving, giving, praying, and I made a commitment to serve God. I did this for 13 years consistently.

During this time the Lord told me to start preparing to move. We lived in that location for 10 years. I wasn't sure I wanted to move, but He told me to give away everything we owned except our living-room furniture. I wondered about the reasoning behind giving it all away. Maybe because I never had sex on the living-room furniture I got to keep it. God never said why.

We moved to a new place where I met an officer, and we started a relationship, which went on for about three years. One day a church elder found out we were in a relationship.

Her words cut deep. "Is that all the worth you have in

yourself—to sleep with another woman's husband?"

Giving him up wasn't immediate. But each time we were together, conviction bore down on me hard. Over time, I stopped seeing him altogether.

Eventually, the Lord asked me to start fasting and praying. I did. Joining the prayer team at church, I was very adamant about learning how to pray and learning how to hear from God. The Lord starting opening doors for me to hear his voice, and I learned how to trust Him by faith.

One day an elder preached about trusting God. The air conditioner in my apartment kept going out. So, I told my rent lady if it happened again I was moving. Each time I got a job or lost a job I got something better with more pay. So my rent increased. God was building my faith in finances. After I heard her sermon, I looked for a different place.

Her words stuck with me. "If you really trust God, why are you on Section 8?"

I could afford rent, but I feared the very idea of stepping into a better environment.

I found a new place. This time, the Lord told me to give away everything we owned. Everything? Did I trust Him enough to give away everything?

I saw a Hispanic man outside "I'm moving. Do you want my furniture?"

His wife didn't speak English well, but she said, "Oh my God. Thank you, Jesus. Our place is empty. I have been praying and asking God for furniture for my family. We moved into our new place with nothing."

Me? An answer to prayer? Apparently so.

Eventually, I lost contact with Isaiah and his dad, but over a 13-year timespan, I continued looking for him. The Lord told me one day I would see him again.

As God established my faith in Him, He also gradually chipped away at my stony heart.

Filled with hate, selfishness, and bitterness, He had a lot of work to accomplish. How sad that I loved God and helping people but simply could not forgive all of those who hurt me. I lived in a false sense of hope and denial—saved, preaching, leading people to Christ, yet nowhere near healed.

After God allowed us to move into our new place, He blessed me with a small business, We Clean Janitorial Service. I started with a box of cleaning supplies left on my job. My supervisor told me I could have them. With new contracts lined up, we lived in a nice apartment. But I started using pills, which took away the ability to stay focused. I had six months of rent money, but without work coming in, we ran out of money. I called my best friend, and we moved in with her.

On the way to her house, our bed flew off the truck, leaving us with a mattress and box spring. The boys took the mattress, and I took the box spring.

I quickly repented, and God restored us. But not before they repossessed my car. Only food stamps provided the means to eat. In spite of everything, my friend showed kindness to us. While we lived with her, the Lord ministered to me, asking that I fast and pray again.

During that time he cleansed me from whoredom, low self-esteem and self-harm. As crazy as it sounds, I feared success. But God took that fear from me.

The Lord ministered to me by dreams at this point. I dreamed about a dealership and the Lord led the way. I went to get a car. The finance man said my credit was bad from the repo, and he denied the loan.

Discouraged, I wasn't ready to give up. "How about giving me a job? Let me prove myself."

The manager said, "No. You don't have any experience."

Every day for two weeks, I called him. He finally hired me, probably to keep me from nagging him but thinking I wouldn't last. I went from making $12,000 to $54,000.00 a year. Life became hopeful, with a future that looked bright. The Lord told me to start looking for a home. We built our first $150,000 home, and my salary increased to six figures.

With all of those blessings, I should have been whole, but I still wanted Isaiah and a husband. My heart ached for my son and someone who truly loved me. In His kindness, God blessed me with a husband.

Breathing the grace of God in deeply, nothing could go wrong.

Chapter 17

Just when everything seemed perfect, one day, my husband asked me to take all of Isaiah's things out of his room. I had four bedrooms, one set up for Isaiah with everything in it as though he lived there. At the very suggestion, I had a breakdown. Fully entrenched in God's Word, I did not know any feelings of pain. Denial provided a great escape from experiencing emotional pain. As a kid, I learned how to leave my body, and for the first year of our marriage, I lived in that same out-of-body experience.

With so many times of molestation and rape in the past and not using pills or drugs, each time my husband touched me I saw those peoples' faces. Sometimes I smelled their bodies and heard their voices.

How? My husband is a very gentle man. He knew all of the abuse I went through. So he called me early during the day to say I love you. Is it ok if we make love tonight?

Full of fear that I might lose him, I was not honest enough to say, "No, I feel pain every time you touch me. I am experiencing something I can't explain."

A preacher, filled with the Holy Spirit, how could I admit I was not healed?

During our marriage, things got so bad my husband filed for divorce and moved out of the house. But he continued to take care of me.

That first year I bore the pain, sleepless nights, crying when he wasn't home and trying to figure out how was I going to get beyond the pain I felt in my privates every time he looked at me. I didn't even understand why it happened. This gentle, loving man, lover and friend—my husband. And I was not able to say, "I am hurting."

Because I learned to live with trauma, pain and constant conflict, my mind told me life was supposed to be this way. Even though my husband exhibited all the godly attributes anyone expected in our marriage, the broken part of my brain couldn't accept them.

He said things like, "I love you—our bed is clean." He reminded me, "This is a union between us and God. You don't have to be afraid. I will take care of you."

But I didn't hear his words. Instead, I heard, "You're a whore—you don't deserve love."

Unable to deal with the ever-present fears, I isolated, which came easy for me—yet another learned behavior. Instead of talking to my husband and letting him help me, I stayed angry with bitterness gnawing away inside.

He often asked, "What's wrong?"

Instead of talking through the deep roots, I found errors in everything he did.

To fix myself, I bought a bigger Mercedes, more designer clothes—the fanciest and most expensive possible. I sold more cars and drowned myself into serving in the community, so I never had to talk to him—or God. I served in so many ministries I became stagnate in my relationship with God. But even then, I came up with an excuse. "God knows all. He will fix it."

For a long time, I made my children say, "Isaiah, come downstairs. Mom wants you." I developed a false sense of hope, which I called faith. Many times I sat in Isaiah's room and talked to him as if he sat on the bed listening to me. Finally, I cleaned out that room, admitting Isaiah didn't live in our home.

Since the time as a kid locked in the closet, I could envision imaginary people to make myself feel safe and whole. That seemed perfectly normal to me, until my husband said, "There is something wrong with you. You need help."

He monitored my behaviors and told my doctor one day I was up, and the next day I was down. My doctor prescribed Lexapro for depression. No one, not my husband, doctor or anyone knew I took all kind of pills just so I could sleep at night. I convinced two doctors my body hurt so bad it affected my sleep. They prescribed different medications.

While my body physically hurt, it was self-inflicted pain.

Trauma comes in all forms. At that time, I did not realize I suffered from trauma, reoccurring disorder, mixed bipolar disorders. The doctors also labeled my condition schizophrenia. Years earlier, a mental health provider diagnosed me as schizophrenic, saying I would never be able to work or take care of myself.

Several years later, I started having mental breakdowns, which caused me to escape reality and participate when I was at church or serving.

After my husband sent me to the doctor, I wasn't able to tell the truth, keeping my secrets so no one knew I really heard voices. I didn't dare tell anyone about the depression. How could anyone understand? Better to leave it unspoken.

Then a friend and I decided to lose weight. Crack always

made me lose weight, so I chose to start using. Just for one month, I reasoned, not realizing I had a disease of addiction. So, I set the monster loose in mind, body and spirit. For five years, I used drugs off on.

I went to treatment seven times and stayed clean for a while, then for a day. Once I went to treatment, believing I was Queen Sheba. They finally discovered my true identity through my phone number and sent me to a different hospital. Then another time I smoked for seven days, and this guy sent me to the wrong house. Three preachers happened to live in the house. One of them prayed for me, but I just wanted to buy some crack. The final time I went to treatment, I chased down an Arlington police officer on a high-speed chase to another place. The officer took me to Millwood Hospital. With my blood pressure soaring, they rushed me to the hospital. When I woke up, a man sat by my bed in a white uniform with a red cross on his chest. Peace came over me. I went to treatment the last time, finally telling the doctors the truth. All the dirty, nasty, ugly truth of my life spilled out.

"I keep hearing voices. I get so depressed I can't get out of the bed. My husband has to bath me to get ready for church." I took a deep breath and continued. "I was raped and abused so much, I can't stop thinking about it, and it affects me greatly."

The doctors listened as I sobbed through more. "I can't stop thinking about Isaiah, and that he really doesn't live with me, and I don't know where he lives. And I can't stop smoking crack, no matter what I try."

The doctor leaned forward and asked one question. "Fern, are you willing to stop?"

"I want to stop. I really do."

With that, he gave me medications for Mixed Bipolar Disorder, Schizophrenia by induced drugs, depression and a stabilizer that helped control cravings.

Maybe—just maybe—healing might come. With help and the continued process, I finally had hope.

Chapter 18

The mix of medications helped with my healing, but no prescription can completely heal. I knew that without God, I couldn't get well.

He ministered to my mind, and one day my brain started to heal—I literally felt the change. I woke up that morning, and the feeling in my privates no longer existed. My heart, usually as heavy as a giant boulder, weighed nothing. I can't explain how God walked me through the process, but I learned the most important truth. If you continue seeking after Him, He will deliver you.

Although it sounds as if my healing happened overnight, the journey took many years with steep mountains to climb and numerous valleys. Many steps led to my deliverance from crack, starting with much prayer and fasting. Attending church regularly, reading my Bible daily and waking up at night asking God for healing all provided pivotal pieces of the journey. Whenever cravings creep up on me—which they sometimes still do—I start the process over, but I don't use. I have a mentor, sponsor and strong support group, yet I continue the process each day. I am not immune from the possibility of returning to the old lifestyle, but under the grace of a loving God, I can overcome any temptation.

Drugs don't only affect your mind, they also affect your body, and that doesn't change just because you quit using. So, I remain careful about what I eat and drink to monitor my craving and triggers. I learned my triggers—meaning I know what can cause me to use again.

Anger is a powerful trigger and can happen anytime. Sometimes, events trigger it, and the accompanying emotions can even be righteous anger. But I don't allow anger to fester. In addition, I count to 100 before making a decision, or I will say some very mean things. Verbally abusing people reigned as my top coping mechanism from early in my childhood. Thus, I have to think and pray before I say anything, which helps me not to overreact.

On a daily basis, I evaluate all the components of my life. I take inventory to assess the thoughts and emotions circulating through my mind. I write in my journal regularly and don't go around the places where I previously scored.

I used by myself, so people are not a trigger for me. However, I must watch out if I get the grandiosity disorder— meaning when buying too much expensive stuff, I must evaluate why. Buying expensive items can mean I want to cover up hidden actions. People look at the outer appearance and not my behaviors, so keeping myself looking successful and like anything but an addict can mean something. For years, I led a double life, looking perfect on the outside, but using and falling apart internally. In that regard, I am not alone. While some may not be hiding the use of drugs, this same disorder can appear in any person who hides the truth of deeply-guarded secrets.

Isolation is big for me. I must consistently go to meetings because I lived by myself for so long. Even in our marriage, I watch for this one. He's in one room, and I'm in another. So I have to go watch TV with him or expect him to come watch with me. Because I suffer from selfishness, it's very important that I don't take away more than I put in the relationship.

Fear lived with me—a big part of my life. I embraced it and learned how to cope with sheer terror. Every day I tell myself I am not afraid. God taught me how to see good in situations instead of only the evil. My first response to fear changed. Trust the process and you can get through without sabotaging the situation.

We easily blame drugs as the problem. Honestly, drugs only showed the symptoms of my problems. I stopped smoking crack and taking pills and only take prescription medication meant for me. But I also had to change behaviors. The Lord helped me with that too. First, He placed me in an environment where people prayed for me. He showed me a new perspective and the purpose He planned when He created me.

I asked God why He let me live. He showed me a time I was in a shootout. The Cubans had powerful guns, riddling the entire car with bullet holes. But, in the dream, I saw where Holy Spirit light covered all the bullets, so neither the driver nor I got hit. He wrote in a book with his finger, "You Are Chosen. You are Ordained." He reminded me I have to be whole and let the past go in order that He may use me for His purpose.

So, I took the necessary steps to detox my mind. I wrote out my thoughts to determine if they were real or fantasy. I listened to the conversations I had with myself, either in my mind or verbally. If they did not line up with God's Word, then I knew it didn't come from God.

I stopped listening to the words my mother spoke over me and the pain inflicted on me as a child, young adult and even during my years of adulthood. I read in the Word what God says about me and how He feels about me as a person, mother, wife, and most importantly, as His child.

Although Mom dealt drugs, she kept it well-hidden, leading a double life like I did. Full of class, she never appeared as a drug dealer or any kind of user. In spite of some bad decisions, I realized she made choices, trying to give me the best things possible. About three years ago, I went to her house, and we reconciled. All of my life, she did her best to make sure we spent birthdays and holidays together. After reconciling, we spent a great deal of time together.

The remorse Mom carried over all she did and the terrible things that happened to me came out as we talked. The anguish in her heart washed over me, soothing my soul. I apologized for my behavior toward her, especially the bitterness I held in my heart over all the years. Admitting I spent most of my life hating her opened a door between the two of us, and an abundance of healing took place on both sides. While I believed she knew about the awful events in my life, she didn't. I certainly never told her.

What if just once I told Mom what any of those people did to me? I know now she loved me, and as a mother would have done her best to protect me. Neither of us had the power to change the past, no matter how much we wanted to make it all different. But we forgave each other. During the last two years of her life, I became her caretaker, a role I am so thankful I accepted. Without forgiveness on both sides, that wonderful relationship couldn't happen. She taught me about business, helping me become a better entrepreneur.

In a huge step that strengthened my faith, I stopped comparing God to other men and my biological father. He is God—absolute. No one compares to Him. I started to appreciate the life God gave me and accepted that I have no power over the past. But I can do better with my future.

Acceptance came hard for me since my children were born in addiction, and I relapsed after 13 years of being clean. Guilt and shame covered me, and I had to forgive myself for the pain I caused them. Yet, I realized God protected them from everything. He ordained me to survive the choices I made, and everything would work for my good.

Deliverance came even harder for me because I kept trying to figure out how God planned to do it. I remember the first 13 years without cravings or racing thoughts. What was wrong with me knowing how He planned to deliver me? He doesn't always show us how or why He completes His work. The Lord changed my inner being, filling me with love for myself. Only then I found the ability to genuinely love others. Able to receive my deliverance and walk in healing, I studied the Word of God and begin applying it to my life.

Learning love perhaps took the most effort. At one point, I thought buying something for me proved love. My mom bought me every expensive item she could buy. Jay did too, and almost every trick I ever knew threw money at me. But material gifts do not equal love. And most of the time, those purchases came with conditions. They weren't love at all, but a cheap substitution for the real thing. How do you learn love when your experiences provide such a warped definition?

My husband simply loved me—no strings attached.

So, I learned to love through my children and husband. God used them as conduits to teach me how to see His true, unconditional love through those closest to me. Since I did not have a dad, I could not see God as "Dad" or "Father." Yet, He touched, kissed and hugged me through my family. After seeing how they stuck by me, I saw God moving through them to show me He never left me either.

After all this, I finally obtained hope to live, love and serve.

Today I can say God was my Greatness in a Mess. He never left me alone in the physical closet, nor in the closet of my mind.

He saved and delivered me from the hands of the true enemy. I should not be alive today. But God took me from a closet, and opened me to the possibilities of a full life. The past became part of the fiber of my being, not defining me, yet making me a vessel He can use.

You don't have to be a drug addict or experience the terrible traumas I suffered to hide in a closet. But whatever put you there, know if I found a way out, so can you. And that way goes by the name of Jesus.

A Final Word

God restored my life. Today, I am a Peer Support Specialist, helping with substance abuse disorders. I serve faithfully in the community with our church and our Non-Profit Heather H.O.P.E.S. Inc., where we assist ex-offenders to get re-established in the community and help reduce recidivism.

Still married to my loving husband, Willie Jinkins, for 9 years, I graduated from Tarrant County College in December 2018, with plans for transferring to a university in 2019. I cannot express the extreme gratitude for my loving children. Corey, Isaiah and Trenton supported me no matter what, and they suffered through a lot of what's.

God truly restored my life, and I pray this book will lead you to a new or closer relationship with Him through our Lord and Savior, Jesus Christ.

"That if thou shalt confess with thy mouth the Lord Jesus, and shalt believe in thine heart that God hath raised him from the dead, thou shalt be saved. For with the heart man believeth unto righteousness; and with the mouth confession is made unto salvation."

Romans 10:9-10 (KJV)

The verse written above provides the basis for beginning a personal relationship with Jesus Christ. Through Him, any trauma from the past can be healed. Confess with your mouth and believe in your heart that Jesus is who He claimed to be. That's it. Come just as you are and find His love and healing.

If you made this decision for the first time today or recommitted yourself to Jesus, reach out to a local church or trusted Christian friend. Sharing this life-changing decision helps in maintaining a growing relationship with the Lord.

About the Author

Fern Jinkins, Executive Director of Heather H.O.P.E.S. Inc., has spent 21 years serving in the community. Mrs. Jinkins' nonprofit endeavors and experiences have found her working with Teen Mothers and their children, Ex-Offenders and Parolees, and various Faith-based entities through the organization and facilitation of a wide range of administrative responsibilities, strategic planning, volunteer development and fundraising.

For the past five years, Fern Jinkins has served in several leadership roles through Heather H.O.P.E.S., with the development of a Mentor Program for Prison Fellowship with Dawson State Jail, and empowering clients as an Instructor for Substance Abuse, Life Skills, and Anger Management Education Classes. Fern has built relationships and partnerships in the community and created avenues to receive donations for Clothing Drives. She has been an Advocate for the Home of Greater Joy, a Board Member for the Restorative Justice Center, a Liaison and Volunteer Coordinator for the Texas Department of Criminal Justice, and Volunteered for Opening Doors for Women In Need, Salvation Army, Women Who Care Share Fundraiser, and the Butterfly Movement. Through the vision and mission of Heather H.O.P.E.S., Fern has been integral in the establishing of sponsorships and partnerships with Street FX, Walmart, Mt. Sinai Missionary Church, and other volunteers in the community.

Fern Jinkins and Heather H.O.P.E.S., most recent projects and endeavors include the implementation of a Board of Directors, successfully sponsoring the Christmas Give Away and Toy Drive for the Texas Department of Criminal Justice Re-Entry Program and FWISD's New Lives School for Teenage Mothers, and planning Heather HOPES Toy Drive for Lisa's Little Angels.

Fern earned her associates degree from Tarrant County College, graduating in December 2018.

Bio written by,
Topaz Ingram Thornton, Dean of Instruction
Forest Oak Middle School-FWISD
Topaz.Thornton@fwisd.org